"This fascinating and extensive treatment of

organized, meticulously documented, and superbly informative. Although not all of the ancient reports are of equal weight, all are of interest and King has performed a valuable service in thoroughly collecting all of these accounts. His work is especially invaluable for the nineteenth century through the present, where more solid information is available. Practitioners will also appreciate that King has more direct experience with healing ministry than do many of us who have researched the topic." - Craig Keener, Ph.D., author, *Miracles: The Credibility of the New Testament Accounts*

"Having devoted many years to the study of God the Healer, I can say with assurance that this series is one of a kind, an extraordinary tour de force, a labor of great love and learning. Here you will find gathered together a vast array of material on divine healing, both academic and popular, meticulously listed and succinctly summarized. This is a treasure trove for everyone who wants to know more about this critically important subject." - Michael L. Brown, Ph.D., author, *Israel's Divine Healer*

"This series offers a meticulously researched, comprehensive historical survey of Western Christian healing practices. Encyclopedic in its coverage, practitioners and scholars alike will find it a valuable reference guide to primary and secondary sources from the first through the twenty-first centuries." - Candy Gunther Brown, Ph.D., author of *Testing Prayer: Science and Healing*

"Since 1984, I have passionately pursued learning all I could about healing and the healing movements. This book series is the most thorough study on healing movements that I have read. It is a wonderful service to the Protestant churches. I am not aware of any other book in print that is as thorough. Every pastor and evangelist should have this collection in their bookcase." - Randy Clark, D.Min., author, *Authority To Heal: Restoring the Lost Inheritance of God's Healing Power*

"J. D. King has produced what is perhaps the most thorough documentation of Christian healing available. He offers a vast array of primary source material that is of exceptional value for further research. Hence, this work should appear in every serious theological research library as well as in the course syllabi in Church history, practics, and especially systematic theology. The text is indispensable (and highly supportive) for the thousands of burgeoning missions schools serving the 700 million Pentecostal/charismatic constituency around the world. I heartily commend this book to anyone seeking an exhaustive and sympathetic history of Christian healing--a central element in what the New Testament describes as the "good news" (Romans 15:18-20)." - Jon Ruthven, Ph.D., author, *On the Cessation of the Charismata*

"Once in a while, I come across something that goes beyond a surface view of the history of revival and offers us a deeply rich historical account. This book series is one of those rare books. Every Christian who seeks to not only understand but move daily in the power of the Holy Spirit needs to read these books. When we know the long, established history we have inherited from those who have gone before us, and sacrificed so much, we are inspired and "re-fired" to carry on the great fight of faith and bring the gospel of God's kingdom to the world in all His grace, love, and power." - Roberts Liardon, author, *God's Generals*

"I am very pleased to see J.D. King's work in print. Its detailed coverage of the many manifestations of Christ's healing power through His church is a much-needed addition to the corpus of the literature of Christian healing. Here in one work, all the major (and even some minor) Christian healing movements and figures are described. This is a wonderful resource for any Christian and especially for those in the healing and deliverance movement." - William L. Dearteaga, Ph.D., author, *Quenching the Spirit, and Agnes Sanford and Her Companions: The Assault on Cessationism.*

"I have known J.D. King for over four years and have appreciated his heart of passion for researching the roots of the ministry of healing in the church, from the ministry of Jesus to present day. This book series is the fruit of years of labor on this topic, and is undoubtedly, the most exhaustive approach to this subject that I have encountered. You will feel the author's heartbeat for the present day church to stand on the strong foundations for the ministry of healing that are not an accessory of the gospel of the Kingdom, but essential for the gospel to be fully expressed and received. This will be a great resource for our Global School of Supernatural Ministry, as well as the other education programs at Global Awakening." - Mike Hutchings, Ph.D., Director Global School of Supernatural Ministry

"It is with great pleasure that I recommend this book series by J.D. King. This exhaustive work presents readers with an excellent overview of the divine healing movement throughout church history. It uses critical analysis and insightful biographical narratives to recount the significant stories of the pioneers and leaders of the movement. The work is supported with sound documentation consisting of both primary and secondary sources. While it will certainly be useful to scholars, it will also be appreciated by students, ministers, and laity. One important feature of this research is the attention that King gives to the controversies and extremes surrounding the divine healing movement. In short, he leaves no stone unturned. Through this work, King has shown himself to be a true scholar and solid historian of church history. Well done!" - Roscoe Barnes III, Ph.D., author, *F.F. Bosworth: The Man Behind 'Christ the Healer'*

"Salvation encompasses concerns of both body and soul, individual and society, the material and the spiritual. It is inclusive of conversion, social concerns, healing, deliverance and even the regeneration of the universe."[1]

– CLARK PINNOCK AND ROBERT BROW

---

1. Clark H. Pinnock and Robert Brow, *Unbounded Love: A Good News Theology for the 21st Century* (Eugene, Oregon: Wipf and Stock, 1994), 112.

Healing in History

VOLUME TWO:

MEDIEVAL

(600 - 1500)

J.D. King

Christos

Printed in the United States of America
First Printing, 2019

Originally published in *Regeneration: A Complete History of Healing in the Christian Church, Volume One*, Lee's Summit, MO: Christos Publishing, 2017.

ISBN 978-1-950053-00-1

Christos Publishing
P.O. Box 1333
Lee's Summit, Missouri 64063

Cover image is a painting by Domenico Beccafumi, Catherine of Siena Receiving the Stigmata (1515). It was generously provided by J. Paul Getty Museum, 1200 Getty Center Drive, Los Angeles, CA 90049-1679.

Layout by Rachel Greene

Table of Contents

Acknowledgements

A work of this nature cannot be birthed without the assistance of a multitude of people: family, associates, and friends. My debts of gratitude for all the help that I have received are extensive. I want to specifically thank Carole Hawkins, Rachel Greene, and Shawn Jonas.

It is also important to acknowledge my wife, Bobbie, and our wonderful children, Allyson and Matthew. Your unwavering support for me as this project persisted over several years has truly meant the world to me. I love you!

Introduction

For as long as I can remember, I have had an interest in divine healing. I will never forget the scorching summer healing services I attended as a child. Under the hot, musty tent I watched flamboyant evangelists pray for the sick. The sights and sounds that took place under those dangling lights still weave a rich tapestry of fervor and deep-seated human emotion within me.

Once, I caught sight of a frail housewife teetering on the edge of collapse. I watched as she made her way on frail, feeble legs to the front. I observed the old evangelist praying for her. As soon as prayer exploded from his mouth, I knew something unusual was transpiring.

In the split second before the crowd erupted, the makeshift boards on the platform bent and squeaked. Suddenly, a sound of praise erupted from the woman's lips: "Oh, thank you, Jesus!" Virtually every person in the tent stood to his or her feet, praising God and shouting and lifting their hands as this woman pranced up and down. To my youthful eyes, witnessing this woman's healing was overwhelming.

Likewise, I will never forget sitting near the aisle in a tent meeting when a tall, lanky man inched to the front. Apparently, for several years this hard-working farmer had been experiencing excruciating pain in his lower back. As he slowly crept forward, grunting and writhing, severe spasms appeared to overtake him. However, when the evangelist laid his sweaty hands on this man, it became apparent that something was happening. You could just feel it in the air.

Everyone in the tent froze as the man slowly reached downward. Little by little, he bent farther and farther towards the floor. The people watched in amazement as this once-aching man reached all the way down and touched the floor. Then, at the evangelist's urging, the man raised himself and repeated the procedure while the elated multitude gasped.

In the crowded background of this great drama, one could hear piercing shouts of hallelujah, thunderous clapping, and clamoring tongues. As healing was manifested, the crowd exploded with elation. Even I could not resist the overwhelming sense of joy that pervaded that old, musty tent on that warm evening.

The past catches up with us in unexpected ways and places

These experiences gripped my imagination, causing me to hunger for more of Jesus. Though I faced many challenges and even struggled with my faith as I grew older, I could never shake what I had witnessed. The first-hand experiences of healing were what carried me through difficult times and kept me from walking away from the faith. Because of what I had seen, I could never question the reality of Jesus. Historian Diarmaid MacCulloch aptly declared, "the past catches up with us in unexpected ways and places."[1]

As I aged, I longed to relive those stirring moments of fervor from my childhood! So, dusty books with broken spines and foxed pages became something of a time machine. While journeying through their brittle, yellow pages, I became acquainted with forgotten movements and disinherited men.

As I discovered withered paperbacks and beat up hardcovers in second-hand bookshops, I encountered unrecognized leaders and movements. Although familiar with the Pentecostal-Charismatic movement, other traditions were outside my expertise. I honestly didn't expect to find this fervor embedded in other denominations, but I did.

I remember how astounded I was as I learned that healing was a prominent liturgical practice within Roman Catholicism

---

1. Diarmaid MacCulloch, All Things Made New: The Reformation and Its Legacy (New York: Oxford University Press, 2016), 5.

until the ninth century. I also didn't expect to find it being expressed so vigorously throughout the Middle Ages.

When it was demonstrated that Martin Luther, John Wesley, and Charles Spurgeon prayed for the sick, I was astounded. Similarly, I was stunned at the assertion that healing has been actively expressed in the Anglican communion since the early twentieth century. It was also brought to my attention that healing was an undercurrent within evangelicalism. This truth was so counterintuitive that I was hesitant to accept it.

The fact that God has moved through "Spirit-filled" people has been extensively documented. What is less known is that He has also worked through monastics, reformers, Quakers, Methodists, and Presbyterians. Through innumerable expressions and traditions, Jesus has persistently touched the infirmed. With an overview of history in mind, James Opp suggests that "faith healing as a cultural practice itself shifts across different groups over time."[2]

Healing is a Fundamental Expression of Christianity

In my studies, I observed that healing has remained a fundamental expression of Christianity. It has colored the

---

2. James Opp, The Lord For The Body: Religion, Medicine, and Protestant Faith Healing in Canada 1880-1930 (Montreal, Quebec: McGill-Queen's University Press, 2007), 12.

gospel experience for multitudes. Even in darkest periods, physical deliverance continued to be fervently expressed. It is an indisputable expression of the church. Reflecting on this, Amanda Porterfield writes

> Healing is a persistent theme in the history of Christianity, threading its way over time through ritual practice and theological belief, and across space through the sprawling, heterogeneous terrains of Christian community life and missionary activity. To focus on healing in the history of Christianity . . . is to attend to important elements of continuity amid the jumble of competing doctrines, innumerable churches, disparate behaviors, and historical developments.[3]

Porterfield continues, noting, "Although I was prepared to take the reality of Christian healing seriously, I did not expect to find the history of Christianity so laden with its signs."[4] Beneath divergent backgrounds and conflicting theologies, the contours of an incredible story can be traced.

---

3. Amanda Porterfield, Healing in the History of Christianity (New York: Oxford University Press, 2005), 3.

4. Ibid. Kenneth Mackenzie. st. New York: 87.ess, Publishing, s,sity Press, 2006), 3. was autobiographical and historical. The quality

Comprehending The Wondrous Works of God

The History of Healing Series is a multi-volume collection that explores the works of God through numerous Christian traditions. It explores how physical deliverance has been understood and encountered.

I hope that through this series, the significance of healing will be grasped. If the older accounts are carefully studied, people will be better positioned to comprehend the wondrous works of God.

Stupendous healing stories not only help us reconcile the past, they are also a catalyst for the future. Søren Kierkegaard declared, "Life must be understood backward, but … it must be lived forwards."[5]

---

5. Søren Kierkegaard, Journals and Notebooks, Volume 4, JNB-NB5 (Princeton, New Jersey: Princeton University Press, 1843, 2011), 164.

CHAPTER ONE

Overview

"Remember the days of old; consider the generations long past. Ask your father and he will tell you, your elders, and they will explain to you." (Deuteronomy 32:7)

As Christianity stumbled into the tumultuous middle ages, healing remained a vital concern. Believers continued to "express their faith in the ongoing healing power of Christ and to distinguish Christian heroism in the face of sickness and death from pagan fear."[1] Nevertheless, the practice began to modify. Ronald Kydd acknowledges

---

1. Amanda Porterfield, *Healing in the History of Christianity* (New York: Oxford University Press, 2005), 47.

Healing extended throughout this period, but surrounding its practice and permeating its theory was a confusing, multi-faceted diversity. The church lived in change, prayed in change, and occasionally healed in change.[2]

Reflecting on the diversity of experiences, Amanda Porterfield declares

As Christianity spread into different parts of the ancient world, belief in the healing power of Christ came to expression in numerous ways. In Syria and Egypt, holy men withdrew from society to fight demons and prepare their bodies for Christ and attracted streams of visitors to their outposts, eager to be cleansed and healed. In urban environments, Christians banded together for worship services that incorporated exorcism and healing along with other practices that strengthened individuals through union with Christ and with one another as members of his collective body in this world.[3]

In the beginning, physical deliverance was predominantly a thaumaturgical[4] expression. Barrett-Lennard suggests that

---

2. Ronald Kydd, "Jesus, Saints, and Relics: Approaching the Early Church Through Healing," *Journal of Pentecostal Theology* 1.2 (1993), 104.

3. Amanda Porterfield, *Healing in the History of Christianity* (New York: Oxford University Press, 2005), 44–45.

4. Thaumaturgical is the Greek term for "wonder-working."

Paul's references to individuals with gifts of healings in 1 Corinthians 12:9, 28, 30 provides "evidence of the existence of a charismatic tradition in which individual Christians were understood to have received a particular charism of healing that they exercised among members of their local congregation."[5]

As Christianity expanded throughout the Roman Empire, healing became "associated with the liturgy of the church."[6] It became incorporated into the visual and emblematic worship practices.

---

5. See Ric Barrett-Lennard, "The Canons of Hippolytus and Christian Concern with Illness, Health, and Healing" *Journal of Early Christian Studies* 13:2, 142.

6. Avery Brooke, *Healing in the Landscape of Prayer* (Boston: Cowley Publications, 1996), 21.

CHAPTER TWO

Eucharistic Healing

Early Christians pursued healing through the sacrament of Holy Communion. Church leaders often highlighted "the miraculous qualities of the Eucharist in which Christ became fully present in the consecrated Communion host."[1] As the infirmed partook of the elements, they believed that they were more than mere emblems. In the bread and the wine, they were encountering Jesus' healing presence.

Ignatius of Antioch (35–98) believed that the Eucharist "exerts a healing action."[2] He writes that believers should "gather in one faith . . . in order to obey the bishop and the

---

1. Meredith B. McGuire, *Lived Religion: Faith and Practice in Everyday Life* (New York Oxford University Press 2008), 37–38.

2. Raymond Johanny, "Ignatius of Antioch" *The Eucharist of the Early Christians*, trans. Matthew J. O'Connell (Collegeville, Minnesota: The Liturgical Press, 1990), 61.

presbytery, breaking one bread which is a remedy . . . preventing death and giving life in Jesus forever."[3] Calling this "the medicine of immortality,"[4] Ignatius undoubtedly had more than mere symbolism in mind.

One of the communion prayers contained in the *Didache* (AD 100) affirmed, "You have bestowed a spiritual food and drink that lead to eternal life through Jesus, your servant . . . Lord remember your church and deliver it from all evil."[5] This was derived from an early Jewish blessing in which God was "asked to deliver his people from their enemies and afflictions."[6]

Although there "are no actual accounts in the pre-Nicene literature of healing through receiving the Eucharist,"[7] instances are numerous in later works. In one account, Caesarius (AD 468–542), the bishop of Arles, declared, "As

---

3. Ignatius of Antioch, "Epistle to the Ephesians 20:2," in *The Ante-Nicene Fathers*, ed. Alexander Roberts and James Donaldson (Grand Rapids: Eerdmans, 1953), 1.50–51.

4. Ibid.

5. *The Diadache* 10:3b, 5a referenced in Willy Rordorf, *The Eucharist of the Early Christians*, trans. Matthew J. O'Connell (Collegeville, Minnesota: The Liturgical Press, 1990), 3.

6. Ibid., 11.

7. Andrew Daunton-Fear, *Healing in the Early Church: The Church's Ministry of Healing and Exorcism from the First to the Fifth Century* (Eugene, Oregon: Wipf & Stock, 2009), 95.

often as any sickness comes upon anyone, let him who is sick receive the body and blood of Christ."[8]

This practice is also demonstrated in the fourth-century Byzantine work *The Divine Liturgy of Saint John Chrysostom*. One of the prayers in this compilation declares, "O Lord Jesus Christ our God, let your holy body be my eternal life [and] your precious blood my remission of sins. Let this Eucharist be my joy, health, and gladness."[9]

After ingesting the bread and wine, in the Alexandrian *Divine Liturgy of Saint Mark*, the priest was instructed to affirm the following: ". . . all of us who partake thereof . . . may tend unto faith, sobriety, healing."[10]

Examining early Irish and Scottish Communion rituals confirms a "large number of texts relating to the sick."[11] Eucharistic healing is specifically referenced in the *Book of Mulling* (seventh century), the *Book of Dimma* (eighth century), and the *Stowe Missal* (ninth century), along with the Scottish *Book of Deer* (eleventh century). Each beautiful, hand-copied

---

8. Caesarius quoted in F. W. Puller, *The Anointing of the Sick in Scripture and Tradition, with some Considerations on the Numbering of the Sacraments* (London: Society For Promoting Christian Knowledge, 1904) 67.

9. Referenced in *The Divine and Holy Liturgy of Our Father Among the Saints John Chrysostom Archbishop of Constantinople* (Eparchy of Newton, 2009), 92.

10. "The Divine Liturgy of the Holy Apostle and Evangelist Mark, the Disciple of the Holy Peter," *Ante-Nicene Fathers*, Volume 7, ed. Alexander Roberts and James Donaldson (New York: Charles Scribner's Sons, 1899), 558.

11. John Hennig, "Liturgy, Celtic," *Dictionary of the Middle Ages*, Volume 7, ed. Joseph Reese Strayer (New York: Charles Scribner's Sons, 1986), 614.

manuscript presents a variation of the following Communion formula: "May the body with the blood of our Lord Jesus Christ be health for you unto eternal life."[12]

In this period, there was an unmitigated hope for recuperation through the church's liturgy.

---

12. Frederick S. Paxton, *Christianizing Death: The Creation of a Ritual Process in Early Medieval Europe* (Ithaca, New York: Cornell University Press, 1990), 81.

CHAPTER THREE

Baptismal Healing

As the church advanced, healing was not only identified with the "Eucharist but also in the baptismal rite."[1] Daunton-Fear reiterates that, in this early period, "baptism itself was sometimes the means by which a serious illness was cured."[2] Many believed that the water enabled "spiritual healing and the restoration of the divine image that had been lost through sin."[3]

A reference to baptismal healing is embedded in *The Odes of Solomon* (AD 100). This work suggests that the afflicted will

---

1. Avery Brooke, *Healing in the Landscape of Prayer* (Boston: Cowley Publications, 1996), 21.

2. Ibid.

3. Robin Jensen, *Baptismal Imagery in Early Christianity: Ritual, Visual, and Theological Dimensions* (Grand Rapids: Baker Academic, 2012), 27.

be restored after their emergence from the baptismal waters.[4] It affirms that "even lives that were about to expire . . . have been seized from death. And members who have fallen . . . have been restored and set up."[5]

An indication of this form of healing is also evidenced in the *Privileges of the Baptized*, a fourth-century Clementine homily.

> In the present life, washing in a flowing river, or fountain, or even in the sea, with the thrice blessed invocation, you shall not only be able to drive away the spirits which lurk in you; but yourselves no longer sinning, and undoubtedly believing God, you shall drive out evil spirits and dire demons, with terrible diseases, from others. And sometimes they shall flee when you but look on them. For they know those who have given themselves up to God.[6]

---

4. "A renewed physical life was expected for the believer along with new spiritual life through the administration of baptism." Andrew Daunton-Fear, *Healing in the Early Church: The Church's Ministry of Healing and Exorcism from the First to the Fifth Century* (Eugene, Oregon: Wipf & Stock, 2009), 44.

5. Ode 6:15–16, referenced in Andrew Daunton-Fear, *Healing in the Early Church: The Church's Ministry of Healing and Exorcism from the First to the Fifth Century* (Eugene, Oregon: Wipf & Stock, 2009), 42.

6. Pseudo-Clementine Literature, 9.19.4–5, *Ante-Nicene Fathers*, Volume 8, in Andrew Daunton-Fear, *Healing in the Early Church: The Church's Ministry of Healing and Exorcism from the First to the Fifth Century* (Eugene, Oregon: Wipf & Stock, 2009), 122.

Transformation in the baptismal fount is also demonstrated in Augustine's *The City of God* (422). Recounting the story of a physician afflicted with gout, Augustine writes

> A physician in the same town, much troubled with gout . . . [was] baptized . . . [and] freed both from his pain and the cause thereof, so that he never had gout in all his days after. Who knew this man? We did and a few of our neighbor brethren; otherwise it had been utterly unknown.[7]

It was not uncommon to initiate sickbed baptism—where the leaders would immerse those who were severely ill.[8] Cyprian referenced it in one of his epistles.[9]

During these early baptisms, ecclesiastical leaders would, for example, narrate how Naaman was healed when he dipped himself in the Jordan River (2 Kings 5:1–19)[10] and a blind man

---

7. Augustine, *The City of God*, Volume 2, Book 22.8, trans. John Healey (Edinburgh: John Grant, 1909), 340.

8. See Robin Jensen, *Baptismal Imagery in Early Christianity: Ritual, Visual, and Theological Dimensions* (Grand Rapids: Baker Academic, 2012), 27.

9. Cyprian, Epistle 75.13.1.

10. Origen declared, "Realize that those who are covered with the filth of leprosy are cleansed in the mystery of baptism by the spiritual Elijah, our Lord and Savior. To you he says, 'Get up and go into the Jordan and wash, and your flesh will be restored to you.' When [Naaman] washed, he fulfilled the mystery of baptism, and his flesh became like the flesh of a child. Which child? The one who is born in the washing of rebirth." Origen, Homiliae in Lucam 33.5, trans. Lienhard, Origen, 136, in Robin Jensen, *Baptismal Imagery in Early Christianity: Ritual, Visual, and Theological Dimensions* (Grand Rapids: Baker, 2012), 25.

restored after washing in the pool of Siloam (John 9:1–7). Biblical accounts such as these imply that ritual cleansing brings a revocation of sin and bodily cure.

Healing was a common theme in baptistery inscriptions and imagery. An epigram from the Titlis Damasi church, associated with Damascus I (305–384), declares, "This glorious spring contains the waters of health."[11] The Dura Europos church in Syria—one of the earliest surviving sanctuaries—had in its baptismal chamber a painting of the New Testament account of the healing of a lame man.

Evidence suggests that healing was the anticipated outcome for the Ante-Nicene followers of Jesus. For many, post-baptismal disease was as false a situation as post-baptismal sin, and, although there were examples of both, neither was normal in the regenerate life, and both were ideally impossible.[12]

Yet, outcomes would vary, depending on the recipient's faith and the spiritual atmosphere of the room. In one of his homilies, Ambrose of Milan (340–397) acknowledged

> Not all water cures, but only the water that has the grace of Christ cures. Its substance is different from

---

11. Inscription found in De Rossi, Inscriptiones Christianae Urbis Romae 2.135.6, edited by J. B. de Rossi, Rome, 1857–1858. Referenced in Robin Jensen, *Baptismal Imagery in Early Christianity: Ritual, Visual, and Theological Dimensions* (Grand Rapids: Baker, 2012). 24.

12. Evelyn Frost, *Christian Healing* (London: A. R. Mowbray, 1949), 226.

its effect. The work belongs to the water, the effect
of the Holy Spirit. The water does not heal unless
the Holy Spirit descends into it and consecrates it.[13]

Though "little publicized," healing encounters through baptismal waters "may well have occurred throughout church history."[14]

In the post-apostolic period, Christian rites became an avenue for a breakthrough. For centuries, a "significant number of healings were linked to the sacraments of baptism and the Eucharist."[15] Healing was extended through the rhythm and forms of the church.

---

13. Ambrose, De Sacramentis 1.15 (SC 25:68), in Robin Jensen, *Baptismal Imagery in Early Christianity: Ritual, Visual, and Theological Dimensions* (Grand Rapids: Baker, 2012), 26.

14. Andrew Daunton-Fear, *Healing in the Early Church: The Church's Ministry of Healing and Exorcism from the First to the Fifth Century* (Eugene, Oregon: Wipf & Stock, 2009), 152. Baptismal healing transpired, "though it seems to have been little publicized."

15. Michael J. McClymond, "Charismatic Gifts: Healing, Tongue Speaking, Prophecy, and Exorcism," in *The Wiley-Blackwell Companion to World Christianity*, ed. Lamin Sanneh and Michael J. McClymond (West Sussex, United Kingdom: John Wiley and Sons, 2016), 404.

CHAPTER FOUR

Sacramental Healing

As sacramental practices gained a deeper rooting, the ministry of healing obtained a few of its own distinctions. In time, the anointing of the sick developed into a separate rite.[1]

Linda Malia points out that "while there is no indication of an official liturgy" in the first two hundred years

> by the third century we find in an early liturgical treatise known as *The Apostolic Tradition* . . . a

---

1. See John Gunstone, *Healing Power: What It Is and What to Do with It* (Ann Arbor, Michigan: Servant Books, 1987), 58. R. J. S. Barrett-Lennard writes, "It is clear that the practice of healing and even anointing with oil was not restricted during the first five centuries to persons exercising the function of or holding the title of presbuteros. Alongside the ministry of healing, which was exercised by official representatives of the churches, there appears to have been a parallel and related tradition carried out by people who have been recognized by the church as having a particular gift of healing." R. J. S. Barrett-Lennard, *Christian Healing After the New Testament* (Lanham, Maryland: University Press of America, 1994), 57.

prayer for the blessing of oil of the sick, the earliest
example available of such a prayer.[2]

About a century later, a reference to the preparation of oil
for curative purposes is indicated in the *Sacramentary of
Serapion*. This church order declares that "the blessed oil was
held to be a medicament of life and salvation, unto health and
soundness of soul and body and spirit, unto perfect well-
being."[3] Healing by ceremoniously anointing with oil grew
prominent.[4]

Reflecting on the particulars, Amanda Porterfield
observes

> Christians adopted a simple rite, based on
> descriptions of healings Jesus performed, of
> anointing the sick with oil in the name of the Lord.
> Anointing the sick on the lips, ears, and eyes, where
> demons could enter, early Christians performed
> rites "to guard the flesh as a temple of God."[5]

---

2. Linda M. Malia, *Healing Touch and Saving Word: Sacraments of Healing,
Instruments of Grace* (Portland, Oregon: Pickwick Publications, 2013), 28.

3. Ibid.

4. R. J. S. Barrett-Lennard confirms that "there is a considerable body of
evidence referring to the practice of anointing with oil for healing." R. J. S. Barrett-
Lennard, *Christian Healing After the New Testament: Some Approaches to Illness in the
Second, Third, and Fourth Centuries* (Lanham, Maryland: University Press of America,
1994), 55.

5. Amanda Porterfield, *Healing in the History of Christianity* (New York: Oxford
University Press, 2005), 47.

Apparently, this recuperative practice was not confined to church officials. Some of the laity functioned in it as well. Barrett-Lennard writes

> It is clear that the practice of healing or even anointing with oil was not restricted during the first five centuries to the person exercising the function of or holding the title of presbyters. Alongside the ministry of healing, which was exercised by official representatives of the churches, there appears to have been a parallel or related tradition carried out by people who have been recognized by the church as having particular gifts of healing.[6]

Within a relatively short period, physical deliverance became a part of the rites and religious order of the emerging Roman Catholic Church.[7]

---

6. R. J. S. Barrett-Lennard, *Christian Healing After the New Testament: Some Approaches to Illness in the Second, Third, and Fourth Centuries* (Lanham, Maryland: University Press of America, 1994), 57.

7. "I believe that we can safely conclude that prayer and anointing with oil for healing was practiced in diverse geographical areas of the Catholic Church in the first three centuries." R. J. S. Barrett-Lennard, *Christian Healing After the New Testament: Some Approaches to Illness in the Second, Third, and Fourth Centuries* (Lanham, Maryland: University Press of America, 1994), 55.

CHAPTER FIVE

The Rise of the Monastics

Changes were on the horizon, and followers of Jesus were forced to reassess long-held assumptions. Once a persecuted minority, believers finally emerged from the shadows of the catacombs after 313. The brutal Roman Empire abandoned its sword and seemingly embraced the faith. The formerly oppressed were no longer in need of miracles to survive. This created a crisis of identity. Francis MacNutt writes

> In the early days of Christianity, healing and deliverance showed that there was only one true God who was demonstrably more powerful than the false gods of the pagans—who were identified with demons. Miracles also identified Jesus as the long-awaited Messiah. But when Christianity saw

itself as triumphant, the need for miracles as proof died out.[1]

Changes orchestrated fierce disruptions. Due to rising moral and spiritual concerns, some of the devoted no longer wanted to associate with the "institutional church." Christianity's favored status within the Empire had many repercussions on both religious and political life. It was no longer the church of the martyrs, and without the threat of martyrdom, it became much easier to be a Christian. As the churches were flooded with casual Christians, healing became less frequent. Some Christians who were attempting to keep alive the spirit of martyrdom and sacrifice drew apart to live a life of prayer in the deserts of Syria and Egypt.[2]

Nevertheless, separatists upheld the ministry of prayer and deliverance. MacNutt observes that as "more nominal Christians appeared in the churches," fervent Christians, like the desert hermits, were compelled to flee their company and form new, idealistic communities.[3]

---

1. Francis MacNutt, *The Healing Reawakening: Reclaiming Our Lost Inheritance* (Grand Rapids: Chosen Books, 2006), 89.

2. Avery Brooke, *Healing in the Landscape of Prayer* (Boston: Cowley Publications, 1996), 19.

3. Francis MacNutt, *The Healing Reawakening: Reclaiming Our Lost Inheritance* (Grand Rapids: Chosen, 2006), 92.

These separatists were known as monastics, and their "asceticism sometimes gained them a reputation."[4] Some believed that their "personal sacrifice and asceticism led to sanctity, which was manifested in healing."[5] Since they were "regarded as individuals able to work miracles,"[6] it is no surprise that physical deliverance is documented in "the earliest documents associated with monasticism."[7]

Antony of Egypt

Perhaps the most illustrious ascetic was Antony of Egypt (251–356), the beloved father of monasticism. During his teenage years, he gave away his inheritance and retreated to the desert. Antony's experiences over the next 85 years contributed to the institution of monasticism.

The sick and afflicted traveled to the secluded point where Antony resided. Through his fervent prayers, "the Lord healed

---

4. Craig S. Keener, *Miracles: The Credibility of the New Testament Accounts* (Grand Rapids: Baker, 2011), 370.

5. Philip Jenkins, *The Lost History of Christianity: The Thousand-Year Golden Age of the Church in the Middle East, Africa, Asia-and How it Died* (New York: HarperOne, 2008), 75.

6. W. H. C. Frend, *The Rise of Christianity* (Philadelphia: Fortress Press, 1984), 575.

7. Amanda Porterfield, *Healing in the History of Christianity* (New York: Oxford University Press, 2005), 48.

the bodily ailments of many present."[8] Athanasius writes that
Antony

> healed not by commanding, but by prayer and
> speaking the name of Christ. So that it was clear to
> all that it was not he himself who worked, but the
> Lord who showed mercy by his means and healed
> the sufferers. But Antony's part was only prayer and
> discipline, for the sake of which he stayed in the
> mountain, rejoicing in the contemplation of divine
> things, but grieving when troubled by many
> people.[9]

Multitudes "came to learn from him, and healing
deliverance was experienced even by those who waited outside
his cell and did not come into his immediate presence."[10] His
prayers were so efficacious that Athanasius,[11] (296–373)

---

8. Athanasius, *Life of Antony*, in *Nicene and Post-Nicene Fathers of the Christian Church, Second Series*, Volume Four, Ed. Phillip Schaff and Henry Wace (Grand Rapids: Eerdmans, 1978), 200.

9. Ibid., 84.

10. Stanley Burgess, Gary McGee, "Signs and Wonders," *New International Dictionary of Pentecostal-Charismatic Movements*, ed. Stanley Burgess, Gary McGee (Grand Rapids, Michigan: Zondervan, 2002), 1064.

11. Athanasius (296–373) was bishop of Alexandria and referred to as the "Father of Orthodoxy." After receiving an education under the tutelage of the bishop of Alexandria, he went into the desert to spend time with Antony. He later assisted the bishop of Alexandria at the historic Council of Nicaea, where he fashioned his legacy. In addition to his doctrinal and ecclesiastical endeavors, Athanasius ministered healing. It was recently noted that "Athanasius . . . became famous during his lifetime for bringing deliverance to those possessed by evil spirits, the blind, the incontinent,

declared that Antony was "a physician given to Egypt by God."[12]

In one specific account, Athanasius writes

> Fronto . . . an officer of the Court . . . had a terrible disease, for he used to bite his own tongue and was in danger of injury to his eyes. Having come to the mountain, [he] asked Antony to pray for him. But Antony said to him, "Depart, and you shall be healed." But when he was violent and remained there several days, Antony waited and said, "If you stay here, you cannot be healed. Go, and when you enter into Egypt, you shall see the sign wrought in you." And he believed and went. And as soon as he set eyes on Egypt, his pain ceased, and the man became whole according to the word of Antony, which the Savior had revealed to him in prayer.[13]

the deaf and dumb, and those afflicted with cancer. Even after his death, it was reported that the ill were cured when praying at his grave." Stanley Burgess, Gary McGee, "Signs and Wonders," *New International Dictionary of Pentecostal-Charismatic Movements*, ed. Stanley M. Burgess and Eduard M. van der Maas (Grand Rapids: Zondervan, 2002), 1064.

12. Athanasius quoted in R. J. S. Barrett-Lennard, *Christian Healing After the New Testament: Some Approaches to Illness in the Second, Third, and Fourth Centuries* (Lanham, Maryland: University Press of America, 1994), 184.

13. Athanasius, *Life of Antony*, in *Nicene and Post-Nicene Fathers of the Christian Church, Second Series*, Volume Four, Ed. Phillip Schaff and Henry Wace (Grand Rapids: Eerdmans, 1978), 57.

There is little doubt that Anthony "deplored the popularity his success brought."[14] His sincere yearning was to withdraw from society and spend extended time in intercession. He never imagined himself becoming the prototype of an ascetic healer. Nevertheless, that is precisely what happened.

Hilarion

Among those who emulated Antony, there were an astonishing number of healing references. Hilarion (291–371), an ascetic clad in sackcloth and a cloak of skins, chose to live in seclusion in a barren desert seven miles from the city of Majoma near Gaza. While he never intended to minister to others, many journeyed to the outskirts to receive prayer. The following account reveals astounding breakthroughs:

> A certain woman of Eleutheropolis, finding herself despised by her husband because of her sterility—after fifteen years of married life she had brought forth no children—was the first who dared to intrude upon blessed Hilarion's solitude. While he was still unconscious of her approach, she suddenly threw herself at his knees saying, "Forgive my boldness; forgive my importunity. Why do you turn

14. Andrew Daunton-Fear, *Healing in the Early Church: The Church's Ministry of Healing and Exorcism from the First to the Fifth Century* (Eugene, Oregon: Wipf & Stock, 2009), 141.

away your eyes? Why do you shun my pleas?" . . . He stood still, and finally aware of the woman asked her why she had come and why she was weeping. When he learned the cause of her grief, raising his eyes to heaven, he commanded her to have faith and believe. He followed her departure with tears. When a year had gone by, he saw her with a son.[15]

Hilarion was concerned about the needs of others but did not desire to be bothered during times of prayer and meditation. Reflecting on the difficulty of his spiritual predicament, Wace and Piercy note, "The fame of his sanctity spread rapidly, and he was reputed to be a worker of miracles. Men of all ranks . . . were healed."[16]

Hilarion later went into self-directed exile "in search of solitude."[17] Nevertheless, "wherever he went, his miracles betrayed him."[18]

Jerome recounted some of the healings that took place under Hilarion's ministry. One of the stories he recorded was of a blind woman whose sight was restored:

---

15. Roy Deferrai, *Early Christian Biographies* (Fredericksburg, Pennsylvania: Catholic University Press, 1952), 252–253.

16. Henry Wace and William Piercy, "Hilarion," *A Dictionary of Christian Biography* (Peabody, Massachusetts: Hendrickson Publishing, 1911, 1994), 473.

17. Ibid.

18. Ibid.

Facidia is a hamlet belonging to Rhino-Corura, a city of Egypt. From this village, a woman who had been blind for ten years was brought to the blessed Hilarion, and on being presented to him by the brethren (for there were now many monks with him) affirmed that she had spent all her substance on physicians. The saint replied, "If you had given to the poor what you have wasted on physicians, the true physician Jesus would have cured you." But when she cried aloud and entreated pity, he spat into her eyes, in imitation of the Savior, and with similar instant effect.[19]

In another story, Jerome recounted the following:

A charioteer, also of Gaza, stricken by a demon in his chariot became perfectly stiff, so that he could neither move his hand nor bend his neck. He was brought on a litter but could only signify his petition by moving his tongue, and [he] was told that he could not be healed unless he first believed in Christ and promised to forsake his former occupation. He believed, he promised, and he was healed and rejoiced more in the saving of the soul than in that of the body.[20]

---

19. Jerome, *Life of Hilarion*, 15–16, in *Nicene and Post-Nicene Fathers*, second series, volume 6, ed. Philip Schaff and Henry Wallace (New York: Cosimo Classics, 1893, 2007), 360.

20. Ibid.

Hilarion was an important part of healing's persistence in the expanding monastic tradition.

Theodore of Mopsuestia

Theodore of Mopsuestia (350–429), a Syrian theologian, was a proficient biblical interpreter. As a young man, he was persuaded to enter the ascetic life by Chrysostom. He entered a monastery near Antioch and ultimately became bishop of Mopsuestia in 392.

Theodore once declared, "Many heathen amongst us are being healed by Christians from whatsoever sickness they have, so abundant are the miracles in our midst."[21] From this, it is clear that healing remained a vital means for evangelism and Christian identity.

Palladius of Galatia

Other ascetic accounts indicate the prominence of healing. For example, Palladius of Galatia (363–430), bishop of Helenopolis in Bithynia, compiled brief sketches of the Desert Fathers in a work called *The Lausiac History* (419).

In one instance, Palladius recounts the story of Benjamin, a monastic in the Nitrian Desert of Egypt.

---

21. Theodore of Mopsueste, *Christlieb: Modern Doubt*, 321, in Adoniram Judson Gordon, *The Ministry of Healing* (Whitefish, Montana: Kessinger Publishing, 2006), 62.

Through the laying on of hands and the use of oil,
he had blessed and healed all the sick brought to
him. In this mountain of Nitria, there was a man
called Benjamin who at the age of eighty years,
having reached the perfection of asceticism, was
counted worthy of the gift of healing, so that
everyone on whom he laid his hands or to whom he
gave oil after blessing it was cured of every
ailment.[22]

Palladius' inspiring account is not exceptional. Other
monks were also sharing testimonies of marvelous works.

Theodoret of Cyrrhus

Although conflicted about the miraculous, Theodoret of
Cyrrhus (393–457) uncovered astonishing accounts when
compiling *The History of the Monks of Syria* (428). In this
notable work, he references James of Cyrrbestica, a monastic
who operated in physical deliverance. Theodoret suggested
that James had culled the gifts of divine grace:

Through his blessing, many fevers have been
quenched—and still are—[and] many agues have
abated or departed completely, many demons have

---

22. Palladius, *Lausiac History*, 12.1, *The Lausiac History of Palladius*, Volume 2,
ed. Dom Cuthbert Butler (United Kingdom: Cambridge University Press, 1904), 35–
36.

been forced to flee; and water blessed by his hand becomes a preventive medicine.[23]

In one instance, a grieving father had brought his dead child before James, entreating him to resuscitate the child. Theodoret states

> The man of God, placing the child before him and kneeling down, lay prostrate as he entreated the Master of life and death. In the late afternoon, the child made utterance and called his father. This inspired man, perceiving thereby that the Master had accepted the petition and bestowed life, got up, and after worshipping the one who does the will of those who fear him and hearkens to their requests, completed his prayer and restored the child to his begetter. I myself saw the child and heard the father narrating the miracle; and I have transmitted to many this story worthy of the apostles, knowing that it will be a cause of great benefit to those who hear it.[24]

Theodoret also wrote about a remarkable healing that transpired through a hermit named Peter. An afflicted woman, who could not see out of one eye, had come before this ascetic,

---

23. Theodoret of Cyrrhus, *A History of the Monks of Syria*, 21.14, trans. R. M. Price (Trappist, Kentucky: Cistercian Publications, 1985), 138.

24. Ibid., 138–139.

petitioning him for a breakthrough. Detailing this encounter,
Theodoret recounts

> Seizing his feet and imploring loudly, she begged
> to be granted a cure for her eye. He protested that
> he was a man with the same nature as hers and
> carrying a great burden of sins, which deprived him
> of familiar access to God. When my mother
> besought him with tears and declared she would
> not go away without obtaining the cure, he replied
> that it was God who heals these things and always
> grants the petitions of those who believe: "So now
> too," he said, "will he grant it, not showing favor to
> me but recognizing your faith: so if you have faith
> pure and unmixed and free from all doubt, then,
> bidding farewell to doctors and medicines, accept
> this medicine given by God." Saying this, he placed
> his hand on her eye and, forming the sign of the
> saving cross, drove out the disease.[25]

Although Theodoret expressed doubts about
contemporary works of miracles, he was persuaded that God
had worked through holy men of the recent past. He
understood that this was an important part of the ancient
heritage.

---

25. Ibid., 84.

Hospicius

Hospicius, characteristically clothed in iron chains and a shirt made out of hair, was a lesser-known sixth-century ascetic who also brokered bodily cures. In one instance, he encountered a young man who could not speak or hear. McClymond points out

> Hospicius poured consecrated oil down the young man's throat and grabbed hold of his tongue as he prayed. After receiving healing, the young man realized that he no longer needed to make a pilgrimage to a distant shrine, since he had already received the healing that he sought.[26]

Hospicius, through extraordinary ascetic expressions, demonstrates the vibrancy and glory of Jesus. He is a noteworthy example of healing's continuing consequence.

The Egyptian Monastics

Physical deliverance is also evidenced in papyri fragments recently unearthed in Mesopotamia. Apparently, five letters written to ascetics in fourth-century Egypt "indicate that these

---

26. Michael J. McClymond, *Charismatic Gifts: Healing, Tongue-Speaking, Prophecy, and Exorcism*, in *The Wiley-Blackwell Companion to World Christianity*, ed. Lamin Sanneh and Michael J. McClymond (West Sussex, United Kingdom: John Wiley and Sons, 2016), 404–405.

men were famous for the healing effects of their prayers for the sick."[27]

In one mangled manuscript, a woman named Valeria wrote to a monk named Paphnutius. She believed that his prayers were efficacious. In this letter, she declares

> I am overcome with a serious disease in the form of a terrible difficulty in breathing. For thus I have believed and I continue to believe that if you pray on my behalf, I will receive healing. I ask God, and I ask you also: remember me in your holy intercession.[28]

In written correspondence addressed to Nepheros, a petitioner named Horion exclaimed

> I know, therefore, my lord father, that next to God the Lord, your prayers have made me healthy, and I believe firmly again in God the Lord that,

---

27. Amanda Porterfield, *Healing in the History of Christianity* (New York: Oxford University Press, 2005), 48.

28. The Paphnutius Letters, P. Lond, VI.1926, in R. J. S. Barrett-Lennard, *Christian Healing After the New Testament: Some Approaches to Illness in the Second, Third, and Fourth Centuries* (Lanham, Maryland: University Press of America, 1994), 58.

through your prayers, we will, in the end, be restored to our homes.[29]

In this interchange, Horion references a previous healing that he had experienced. He is convinced that he will have a similar encounter as Nepheros fervently prays for him again.

In a different epistle addressed to Nepheros, a similar request for healing was made. It reads

> For I, Topiam, was sick and still cannot leave my bed. We entreat you, therefore, to pray for our health because previously our children were sick and through your prayers, they recovered. For we believe that the Lord will hear those who are righteous."[30]

These letters can be interpreted

> as evidence that healing played a central role in the emergence of monasticism in Egypt, and that holy men in late antiquity carried forward the performance of healing earlier associated with Jesus and the apostles.[31]

---

29. "The Nepheros Letter," P. Neph, 10, in R. J. S. Barrett-Lennard, *Christian Healing After the New Testament: Some Approaches to Illness in the Second, Third, and Fourth Centuries* (Lanham, Maryland: University Press of America, 1994), 79–80.

30. The Nepheros Letter, P. Neph. 1. Ibid., 71.

31. Amanda Porterfield, *Healing in the History of Christianity* (New York: Oxford University Press, 2005), 48.

Physical rejuvenation through the agency of Jesus continued to be a vital undercurrent among the ascetics.

Venerable Bede

There are other enthralling accounts as well. The Venerable Bede (673–735), the Father of English History,[32] includes stimulating healing extracts in his *Ecclesiastical History of the English People* (731). One finds, for example, Germanus of Auxerre (378–448). Although born in the Celtic region of Western Europe, in later years he became a missionary to Britain.

Germanus conveyed healing to a pagan tribunal leader's ten-year-old daughter who was unable to see. As her eyes were opened, he was able to explain the gospel.[33]

On a separate occasion, one of the sons of the prominent tribal figure Elafius was publicly healed. Bede recounts

> The nerves being withered, his leg was so contracted that the limb was useless, and he could not walk . . . Germanus, causing the youth to sit

---

32. Meesaeng Lee Choi, "Healing," *Encyclopedia of Christianity in the United States*, Volume 3, ed. George Thomas Kurian and Mark A. Lamport (Lanham, Maryland: Rowman & Littlefield, 2016), 1063.

33. This tribunal leader "presented his blind daughter, ten years of age, for the priests to cure . . . Germanus . . . invoked the Trinity, and taking into his hands a casket with relics of saints, which hung about his neck, applied to the girl's eyes, which were immediately delivered from darkness." Bede, *Venerable Bede's Ecclesiastical History of England*, 1:18, ed. J. A. Giles (London: Henry G. Bohn, 1849), 29

down, gently passed his healing hand over the leg that was contracted; the limb recovered its strength and soundness by the power of his touch, the withered nerves were restored, and the youth was, in the presence of all the people, delivered whole to his father.[34]

In Bede's work, one also witnesses Augustine of Canterbury (570–604), a Benedictine monk sent as a missionary to England by Pope Gregory I (540–604). Reporting on the success of this mission, Bede refers to a commendation letter in which the pontiff had celebrated the healings and miracles, acknowledging, "The English, by outward signs, were drawn to inward grace."[35]

What was transpiring must have been substantial because Gregory acknowledged that Augustine operated in "the gift of working miracles."[36] In fact, he warns the missionary not to be "puffed up by the number of them."[37] His efforts were reportedly the catalyst for the widespread acceptance of Christianity in England.

Another distinguished monk that Bede memorialized was Cuthbert (634–687). This ascetic was closely associated with the monasteries of Melrose and Lindisfarne in Northumbria.

---

34. Bede, *Venerable Bede's Ecclesiastical History of England*, 1:21, ed. J. A. Giles (London: Henry G. Bohn, 1849), 33.

35. Bede, *Venerable Bede's Ecclesiastical History of England*, 1:31, Ibid., 57.

36. Ibid.

37. Ibid.

In one account, Cuthbert brought healing to a nun who had been injured while trying to escape an onslaught of marauders. This woman was "oppressed with a grievous sickness, and for a whole year had suffered from intolerable pains in the head and her whole side, so that her case was considered desperate by the physicians."[38] Cuthbert "anointed her with consecrated oil. And immediately, from that hour, she began to revive, and in a few days, was restored to perfect health."[39]

Bede also referenced John of Beverley (died 721), a monastic from Northumbria who "had a remarkable ministry of healing."[40] In one instance a nun named Coenberg, from Wetadun, had severe blood loss in her arm. The limb was not only swollen but also gripped by an intolerable pain. The abbess asked John to come and speak a blessing over this woman. As he spoke words of life, healing took place. The girl declared

> As soon as the bishop had said the prayer, given me his blessing, and gone out, I immediately began to mend; and though I have not yet recovered my former strength, yet all the pain is quite gone from

---

38. Bede, *The Life and Miracles of St. Cuthbert, Bishop of Lindisfarne*, 31, in *Complete Works of Venerable Bede*, Volume 4, ed. J. A. Giles (London: Whittaker and Co., 1943), 307.

39. Ibid.

40. David Allen, *The Unfailing Stream: A Charismatic Church History Outline* (Tonbridge, Kent, United Kingdom: Sovereign World International, 1994), 37.

my arm where it was most intense, and from all my
body as if the bishop had carried it away with him.[41]

On another occasion, John of Beverley also prayed for a
man with aphasia, a disorder that severely affects speech.

> The Bishop . . . caused the poor man to come in to
> him, and ordered him to put his tongue out of his
> mouth and show it to him; then laying hold of his
> chin, he made the sign of the cross on his tongue,
> directing him to draw it back into his mouth and
> speak. "Pronounce some word," said he, "say gae
> (yes)" . . . He immediately said what was ordered."[42]

John of Beverly was filled with "compassion for the poor
and handicapped. On one occasion a man who had injured his
hand and fractured his skull—as a result of falling from his
horse—was fully restored after John had fasted and prayed."[43]

The ascetics that Bede memorialized in his *Ecclesiastical
History of England* reiterate healing's importance to the
missionary expansions of the church.

---

41. Bede, *Venerable Bede's Ecclesiastical History of England*, 5:3, ed. J. A. Giles
(London: Henry G. Bohn, 1849), 239–240.

42. Bede, *Venerable Bede's Ecclesiastical History of England*, 5:2, Ibid., 237–238.

43. David Allen, *The Unfailing Stream: A Charismatic Church History Outline*
(Tonbridge, Kent, United Kingdom: Sovereign World International, England, 1994),
37.

Monastic Healing Kept Islam at Bay

As Islam grew in prominence during the seventh and eighth centuries, gifted monastics initially kept it at bay through displays of the charismata. Philip Jenkins, a leading historian, recognized that "all forms of Christianity, East or West, emphasize charismatic and miraculous themes, to the degree that separated them from the more rationalistic Muslim contemporaries."[44] Islam made no healing claims.

Catholicus Hananishu I (686–700), a Muslim cleric asked a Persian church leader, "What do you think of the religion of the Arabs?" The church leader promptly replied, "It is a kingdom founded on the sword, not a faith confirmed by divine miracles like the Christian faith."[45]

Eliyya, the metropolitan of Nasibin (1000–1049), noted that he had discovered that Christianity was embraced by

> philosophers of the Greeks and their wise men and many peoples and different sects and divers provinces, like the Greeks and the Franks and the Bulgars and the Copts and the Nubians and the Armenians and the Syrians and the Persians and the Turks and the people of China and others of

---

44. Philip Jenkins, *The Lost History of Christianity: The Thousand-Year Golden Age of the Church in the Middle East, Africa, Asia-and How it Died* (New York: HarperOne, 2008), 76.

45. Bar Hebracus, *Ecclesiastical Chronicle* 11:136, in Laurence E. Browne, *The Eclipse of Christianity in Asia: From the Time of Muhammad till the Fourteenth Century* (London: Cambridge University Press, 1933), 80.

the peoples, not from something that they feared or from something that they hoped for; I knew that they could not have entered into it for any other reason than the divine miracles which led them to it.[46]

---

46. Eliyya, the metropolitan of Nasibin, quoted in P. Louis Cheikho, Trois Traites 49, referenced in Laurence E. Browne, *The Eclipse of Christianity in Asia: From the time of Muhammad till the Fourteenth Century* (London: Cambridge University Press, 1933), 83.

CHAPTER SIX

Later Ascetics

Healing was not exclusive to the early monastics. One also discovers testimonies in the narratives of later ascetics.[1] Works of power never really ceased. Those who were separated to God continued to carry forward this transformative ministry.

Bernard of Clairvaux

Stories of physical deliverance were documented in the ministry of Bernard of Clairvaux (1090–1153), the abbot of the

---

1. It is nearly impossible to document every healing reference in the expansive monastic tradition. There are a number of stories like the one that Craig Keener recounted: "The fifth-century Syrian bishop Philoxenus believed that God still granted the charism of healing to some ascetics; healings and exorcisms are also associated with Symeon the Stylite, an ascetic Syrian monk." Craig S. Keener, *Miracles: The Credibility of the New Testament Accounts* (Grand Rapids: Baker, 2011), 367.

Clairvaux monastery and reforming figure in the Cistercian order.

As he exuded spiritual fervor, Bernard encountered disdain. Polite society increasingly found the assertions of "miracle workers" suspect. Bernard's uncle, Gaudry, was not reluctant to share his apprehension:

> More than once he nearly reduced Bernard to tears by telling him that for a man like him to attempt to do miracles was sheer presumption and that, at any rate, there was nothing to them. But one day, Gaudry himself fell seriously ill and at once sent for Bernard and begged him to bless and cure him. "Sorry, my dear Uncle," said Bernard smiling, "I fear I can't do that; it would be sheer presumption for me to attempt any such thing." Whereupon Gaudry pleaded that he had only been trying to save his nephew from pride . . . In the end, Bernard blessed him and cured him both of his illness and of scoffing at his miracles.[2]

Despite opposition, Bernard effectively ministered to multitudes. On one occasion he encountered a deaf and mute boy. After petitioning God for the breakthrough, healing

---

2. Frank C. Darling, *Christian Healing in the Middle Ages and Beyond* (Boulder, Colorado: Vista Publications, 1990) 139–140. Darling drew from Bruno S. James, *Saint Bernard of Clairvaux: An Essay in Biography* (New York, Harper and Brothers, 1957).

transpired. The boy could hear and speak. Bernard placed the boy on a wooden bench and had him address the crowd who had assembled to watch. Many came to faith through this occurrence.

In another instance, Bernard prayed for a child who had been blind from birth. After Bernard had placed hands on this boy, he began to exclaim, "I see day, I see everybody, I see people with hair. My God, now I will no more dash my feet against the stones."[3]

In some of the healing narratives compiled by Abbot Samuel J. Eales, he writes

> The accounts given by these good and trustworthy persons are marvelous enough. The breathing, the touch, the prayer, the benediction of Bernard had wonderful effects. At his voice, the most inveterate complaints disappeared instantly; and entire populations, in many different towns, related with astonishment the cures to which they had been witnesses. Everywhere along the line of his route, the blind regained their sight, the deaf and the dumb heard and spoke, paralytics recovered the use of their limbs, those supposed to be possessed by evil spirits were calmed and restored to reason. To Bernard himself these events were, it would seem,

---

3. Augustus Neander, *General History of the Christian Church*, Volume Four (Boston, Massachusetts: Crocker & Brewster. 1853), 256.

as much a cause of wonder as to anyone. He was frequently known to speak to his intimate friends in this way.[4]

Francis of Assisi

Another distinguished monastic from the later Middle Ages was Francis of Assisi (1181–1226), the celebrated founder of the Franciscan order. Although not inclined to pray for the sick, he would periodically intercede—particularly if children were the ones in need.

In one instance, a paralyzed child was brought to Francis in Toscanella, Italy. Recounting this amazing occurrence, Thomas of Celano wrote the following:

> The boy's father, seeing the man of God was endued with such holiness, humbly fell at his feet and besought him to heal his son. Francis, deeming himself to be unprofitable and unworthy of such power of grace, for a long time refused to do it. At last, conquered by the urgency of the man's entreaties, after offering up prayer, he laid his hand on the boy, blessed him, and lifted him up. And in the sight of all, the boy straightway arose whole in

4. Samuel J. Eales, *St. Bernard Abbot of Clairvaux, AD 1091–1153* (New York: Society for Promoting Christian Knowledge, 1890), 222–226.

the name of the Lord Jesus Christ and began to walk hither and thither about the house.[5]

Bonaventure (1221–1274), a Franciscan theologian and philosopher, compiled accounts of Francis' healing exploits. He wrote that in Narni, Italy, Francis "made the sign of the cross upon a paralytic who had lost the use of his limbs and restored him to perfect health."[6]

This extraordinary monastic also ministered to a woman whose hands were so "contracted and withered" that she could not use them. As soon as Francis "made the sign of the cross over her, in the name of the Lord, she recovered with such perfect health."[7]

Francis later brought restoration to a young boy from Bologna who had become blind by the degeneration of his eyes. Bonaventure states

> one of whose eyes was so darkened by a spot that
> he could see nothing, nor could any remedy effect
> his cure. When the servant of God made the sign
> of the cross over him from head to foot, he so
> perfectly recovered his sight that he soon after

---

5. John Gunstone, *Healing Power What It is and What To Do with It* (Ann Arbor, Michigan: Servant Books 1987), 64.

6. Bonaventure, *The Life of Saint Francis Of Assisi: From the "Legenda Santi Francisci of Saint Bonaventure,"* ed. Henry Edward (London: R. Washbourne, 1868), 155–156.

7. Ibid., 156.

> entered the Order of Friars Minor, and declared
> that he saw better with the eye which had been
> blind than with the other.[8]

Francis "laid on hands to heal the sick" and "is said to have blessed bread that brought healing to those who consumed it. During Francis' lifetime, people cut off pieces of his clothing to use as relics for blessing and healing."[9] In the centuries after his death, he became a legendary figure because of his notable exploits.

Vincent of Ferrer

Sharing the esteem of Francis and Bernard is Vincent of Ferrer (1350–1419), a Valencian Dominican friar. After being critically ill for several years, God healed him and instructed him to minister to the needy. For more than two decades Vincent traveled across Europe, praying for the afflicted.

During Vincent's ministry in the Netherlands, so many remarkable works transpired that "an hour was set aside daily for the healing of the sick."[10] Recounting some of this, Ebenezer Brewer writes

---

8. Ibid., 157.

9. Michael J. McClymond, *Charismatic Gifts: Healing, Tongue-Speaking, Prophecy, and Exorcism*, in *The Wiley-Blackwell Companion to World Christianity*, ed. Lamin Sanneh and Michael J. McClymond (West Sussex, United Kingdom: John Wiley and Sons, 2016), 405.

10. Alban Butler, *Butler's Lives of the Saints*, Volume 2, ed. Herbert J. Thurston and Donald Attwater, Notre Dame, Indiana: Christian Classics, 1956), 32.

> Time would fail us if we told of the sick folk healed
> by St. Vincent Ferrer, the blind he gave sight to,
> the deaf he gave hearing to, the dumb he gave
> speech to, the women he relieved from the pains of
> childbirth, the palsied he restored to strength, and
> the dead he raised to life.[11]

Over the years, Vincent raised up others who were also able to operate in the miraculous. He believed that many among the righteous could express the grace and power of Jesus Christ. Brewer points out

> Vincent employed miracle apprentices or assistants
> to carry on the work when he himself was tired out.
> At such times, he would turn to one of his assistants
> and say, "Today I have done miracles enough and
> am wearied with fatigue. Go now, and do for me
> what is required. God who has bestowed this power
> on me will transfer it for the nonce to you." Four
> hundred sick people recovered their health merely
> by placing themselves on the bed where St. Vincent
> died.[12]

---

11. Ebenezer Brewer, *A Dictionary of Miracles, Imitative, Realistic, and Dogmatic* (Detroit: Gale Research Company, 1966), 150.

12. Ebenezer Brewer, *A Dictionary of Miracles, Imitative, Realistic, and Dogmatic* (Detroit: Gale Research Company, 1966), 237–238.

In his travels, Vincent facilitated over 3,000 miracles, of which 873 were documented at his canonization.[13] He is unquestionably one of the most effective missionaries in the history of Catholicism.

Although healing was practiced throughout the Middle Ages, it became reconfigured over time. Daunton-Fear notes that while the "monks undoubtedly performed great healings,"[14] their methods were "complex and time-protracted, contrasting with the simplicity of earlier years."[15]

Individuals "renowned for their holiness" transacted "dramatic healings." In contrast to the early apostles, their acts of intercession "made full use of consecrated elements." No one was "commanding healing in the name of Jesus."[16]

Medieval healing methodologies were considerably different from the practices of the early apostles. Within time, there would be even more pronounced changes.

---

13. Bert Ghezzi, *Mystics and Miracles* (Chicago: Loyola Press, 2002), 108.

14. Andrew Daunton-Fear, *Healing in the Early Church: The Church's Ministry of Healing and Exorcism from the First to the Fifth Century* (Eugene, Oregon: Wipf & Stock, 2009), 154.

15. Ibid., 143.

16. Ibid., 151.

CHAPTER SEVEN

The Martyr Complex and the Marginalization of Healing

In the years after the official toleration of Christianity, "genuine martyrs . . . would gradually become something of a rarity."[1] Although violent persecution ceased, the "martyr complex" persisted. Some felt the need to initiate "self-flagellation"[2] since the empire was no longer brutalizing followers of Jesus.

---

1. Ronald C. Finucane, *Miracles and Pilgrims: Popular Beliefs in Medieval England* (New York: St. Martin's Press, 1977, 1995), 32.

2. Flagellation or whipping refers, in part, to the flagellation of Jesus prior to his crucifixion. Some Christians have felt the need to literally "mortify the flesh" with self-induced whippings. Some would fling a cattail whip of knotted cords over their shoulders during times of private prayer.

Monastics came to believe that "the perfect Christian life included constant fasting and self-punishments."[3] Some began to deviate from biblical patterns and envisioned sickness as a way to grow in spiritual stamina.

Although the monks "devoted themselves to ordeals of suffering to perfect themselves spiritually," they were willing to occasionally "perform more mundane healings for people who sought them out."[4] They believed that while healing remained an option for the weak, mature believers should learn to withstand the afflictions.

The growing fixation on the "sanctity of suffering" led some to question the value of healing altogether. Some of the monks began to assert that physical deprivation and pain were advantageous. Reflecting on this, Ken Blue noted

> Roman persecution of the church officially stopped during the time of Constantine . . . Without state-sponsored persecution, the true confessors would have to persecute themselves. The self-persecution of the ascetics was inflicted through prolonged fastings, exposure to the elements, sleep deprivation, and the neglect of basic hygiene. Naturally enough, sickness often resulted. So, in the minds of some, sickness became synonymous

3. William DeArteaga, *Quenching the Spirit* (Lake Mary, Florida: Creation House, 1992, 1996), 67.

4. Amanda Porterfield, *Healing in the History of Christianity* (New York: Oxford University Press, 2005), 48.

with the suffering of the true confessors and therefore was viewed positively.[5]

With the legalization of Christianity and martyrdom's cessation in the early fourth century, the idea of self-instituted suffering gained credence. Exposing this disastrous mindset, Francis MacNutt comments

> Fervent Christians began to believe that if God loved you, he would send great sufferings to test you and mark you as a saint. That killed off any desire to pray for healing. If you think that your sickness is sent by God, you will try to patiently endure it rather than to ask God to take it away. If you are a tepid Christian, you might want to get rid of your sickness, but if you are a "real" Christian, you will willingly embrace your sickness as a path to holiness.[6]

In the developing monastic tradition, many began to insist that "whatever requires an undue amount of thought or trouble or involves a larger expenditure of effort . . . must be avoided."[7]

---

5. Ken Blue, *Authority to Heal* (Downers Grove, Illinois: Intervarsity Press, 1987), 23.

6. Francis MacNutt, *The Healing Reawakening: Reclaiming Our Lost Inheritance* (Grand Rapids, Michigan, 2006), 106.

7. Darrel W. Amundsen, *Medicine, Society, and Faith in the Ancient and Medieval Worlds* (Baltimore: Johns Hopkins University Press, 1996), 142.

Since praying for the sick was an intense spiritual endeavor, it should be evaded.

Basil the Great (329–379) acknowledged, "God cured people,"[8] yet insisted that "desperate efforts to cling to life should be renounced by all Christians."[9] It was believed that God is a healer, but a true disciple is not overly concerned with the natural order. The Christian should only look to the spiritual and interior realms. Illustrating this convoluted outlook, Francis of Assisi (1181–1226) affirmed

> If the sick brother . . . persistently demands medicine in his anxiety to restore his body—which is soon to perish and is an energy of the soul—he shows himself to be promoted by the flesh of the devil, and he is unworthy to be one of the brethren because he loved the body better than his soul.[10]

---

8. Amanda Porterfield, *Healing in the History of Christianity* (New York: Oxford University Press, 2005), 53. Drawing from the accounts of the post-Nicene Fathers, John Wimber states, "Eusebius never ceased to wonder at and describe the powers of Basil." John Wimber, *A Brief Sketch of Signs and Wonders Through the Church Age* (Anaheim, California: Vineyard Ministries International, 1984). 15.

9. Amanda Porterfield, *Healing in the History of Christianity* (New York: Oxford University Press, 2005), 53.

10. Francis Assisi quoted in John Gunstone, *Healing Power* (Ventura, California: Servant Books, 1987), 63.

Healing: A Sign of Exemplary Sainthood

Healing undoubtedly continued, but most officials believed that it was dependent on a heightened sanctity and holiness. In one of the contested Clementine homilies, the following was asserted:

> Give me the man who sins not, and I will show you
> the man who suffers not; and you will find that he
> not only does not suffer himself but [also] that he
> is able to heal others.[11]

Within this ethos, ecclesiastical leaders established requirements about what could be said and which gestures could be made while praying. If one ministered without proper authority, that individual could be excommunicated.

Historian Donald Dayton acknowledged that at this time "miracles of healing were relegated more to signs of exemplary sainthood."[12] If you were not deemed morally worthy, you were excluded from this ministry expression.

For centuries, the laity "anointed themselves." However, in the intervening years "the mantle of healer" fell to "the bishops and the other parochial clergy." These officials "were responsible for praying for the sick and consecrating oil for

---

11. "Sins of Ignorance," *The Clementine Homilies 22, Ante-Nicene Christian Library*, Volume 17, ed. Alexander Roberts and James Donaldson (Edinburgh, Scotland: T&T Clark, 1870), 308.

12. Donald Dayton, *Theological Roots of Pentecostalism* (Peabody, Massachusetts: Hendrickson, 1987), 115–116.

anointing them and water for them to drink in church or, if they were chronically ill, at home."[13] Francis MacNutt states

> The anointing came to be seen as a special prerogative of the priest, whose anointing came to be considered as a sacrament—the Anointing of the Sick—which lay people could not minister . . . [In time] healings came to be associated with especially holy people. Instead of the charismatic gifts being seen as ordinary, they came to be seen as rare and as proof that a Christian was deserving of sainthood.[14]

Only a few of the saints were deemed worthy of ministering, and ironically most of them were reluctant to do so. Healing gifts "were seen as tools to be used infrequently because they were a danger to the person's holiness."[15] MacNutt acknowledged that the monks "fled to the desert (AD 400) to escape the sinful cities and then refused, in the name of humility, to pray for the sick."[16]

---

13. Andrew Daunton-Fear, *Healing in the Early Church: The Church's Ministry of Healing and Exorcism from the First to the Fifth Century* (Eugene, Oregon: Wipf & Stock, 2009), 151.

14. Francis MacNutt, *The Healing Reawakening* (Grand Rapids, Michigan: Chosen Books, 2005), 124, 91.

15. William DeArteaga, *Quenching the Spirit* (Lake Mary, Florida: Creation House, 1992, 1996), 66.

16. Francis MacNutt, *The Nearly Perfect Crime* (Grand Rapids, Michigan: Chosen Books, 2005) 11.

John Cassian (360–435), a prominent mystic, began to warn "that it was spiritually dangerous to involve oneself in the ministry of healing."[17] Clarifying this outlook, Cassian penned

> When [the monks] did possess [gifts of healing] by the grace of the Holy Spirit, they would never use them unless perhaps extreme and unavoidable necessity drove them to do so.[18]

The most anointed of that time refused to minister to the sick unless it was absolutely necessary. This was a reconfiguration of the way that the early apostles operated.

Reflecting on this grim, dualistic outlook, Porterfield declared

> Ascetic deprivation and self-inflicted discomfort commanded respect as a path of sanctity throughout early and medieval Christianity. In the late medieval period, mystics developed this tradition of Christian suffering further, employing fasting and other forms of pain and deprivation to celebrate the humanity of Jesus and to identify their own humanity with his.[19]

---

17. Avery Brooke, *Healing in the Landscape of Prayer* (Harrisburg, Pennsylvania: Morehouse Publishing, 2004), 24.

18. John Cassian quoted in William DeArteaga, *Quenching the Spirit* (Lake Mary, Florida: Creation House, 1992, 1996), 67.

19. Amanda Porterfield, *Healing in the History of Christianity* (New York: Oxford University Press, 2005), 101.

Eventually, many of the Christians began to "regard sickness as a discipline sent from God. This change in understanding was a complete reversal of the earlier belief that God sent health and healing power, not illness."[20] The ascetic tradition ultimately reconfigured what was understood about embodiment and well-being.

Sanctity of Suffering

With a blurring of truth, some began to regard illness as a blessing of God. Sickness was no longer considered a manifestation of evil or a perversion of God's good creation. For some, it took on a twisted form of nobility. The outlook shifted from healings to exalting affliction "as a discipline from the hand of God."[21] MacNutt writes

> The tendency of allowing the body to suffer for the sake of the soul was increased when Christianity became popular and when sophisticated intellectuals, indoctrinated by the teachings of the great Plato, became Christian. The entire Greek and Roman cultures were influenced by Plato's thought and this, in turn, affected Christian thought. Plato saw the body as a prison from which

---

20. Avery Brooke, *Healing in the Landscape of Prayer* (Harrisburg, Pennsylvania: Morehouse Publishing, 2004), 24.

21. Craig S. Keener, *Miracles: The Credibility of the New Testament Accounts* (Grand Rapids, Michigan: Baker, 2011), 368.

the soul needed to escape. This devaluing of the body was absorbed into Christianity.[22]

The church deviated from a holistic perspective to embrace the gnostic emphasis on the soul. Illustrating this twisted outlook, Socrates, Plato's influential teacher, once said that he was "entombed in this which we carry about with us and call the body, in which we are imprisoned like an oyster in its shell."[23]

To the Greeks, the body and all its natural accouterments are to be scorned. Rather than believing in the resurrection of the human body, they were concerned with the immortality of the soul. To them, our bodies and all that is natural are cages that entrap our virtuous mind, will, and emotions.

Under this erroneous influence, Christian leaders began to teach that the "body occupies by nature a lower rank in the scale of being than does the soul."[24] They suggested that the "soul is universally superior to the body. No soul can fall so far in sinfulness as to be changed into a body . . . the worst soul is superior to corporeal things."[25]

---

22. Francis MacNutt, *Healing Reawakening: Reclaiming Our Lost Inheritance* (Minneapolis, Minnesota: Chosen Books, 2005), 107.

23. D. H. Trapnell, "Health, Disease and Healing," *New Bible Dictionary*, ed. J. D. Douglas and N. Hillyer (Downers Grove, Illinois: Intervarsity Press, 1982), 455.

24. Vernon Purdy, "Divine Healing," in *Systematic Theology: A Pentecostal Perspective*, ed. Stanley Horton (Springfield, Missouri, Logion Press, 1994), 490–491.

25. Ibid.

As this Greco-Roman outlook grew in acceptance, it did not take long for the diminishment of healing to take place.

CHAPTER EIGHT

Cessationism

As healing waned, its continuance was questioned. Some suggested that when the last of the original apostles and their closest associates died, the gifts of the Spirit were withdrawn. The belief that healing and other charisms ceased functioning in the church is called "cessationism."

In the fifth century, Augustine of Hippo (354–430) began to question post-apostolic healings and miracles. While not the first, he was arguably the most prominent. Communicating a cessationist outlook, Augustine penned the following:

> We have heard that our predecessors, at a stage of faith on the way from temporal things up to eternal things, followed visible miracles . . . When the Catholic Church had been founded and diffused throughout the whole world, on the one hand,

miracles were not allowed to continue until our
time, lest the mind should always seek visible
things, and the human race should grow cold by
becoming accustomed to things which when they
were novelties kindled its faith . . . At that time, the
problem was to get people to believe before anyone
was fit to reason about divine and invisible things.[1]

Although Augustine later changed his mind, his earlier
outlook remained influential. While he ultimately wrote
retractions—clarifying his changing beliefs about healing—
Augustine's initial cessationist views remained prominent in
the Western church ethos. Porterfield points out

Theologians in the West who followed in the path
of Augustine did not embrace miraculous healing
as a manifestation of mystical experience as
straightforwardly as Eastern theologians did.[2]

1. Augustine, "Of True Religion," in *Augustine: Earlier Writings*, trans. John H.
S. Burleigh (Philadelphia: Westminster Press, 1953), 247–248.

2. Amanda Porterfield, *Healing in the History of Christianity* (New York: Oxford
University Press 2005), 23. The ministry of healing has remained a part of the liturgy
and expressions of Eastern orthodoxy. This tradition identifies its roots in the early
church, particularly as it developed within the Greek-speaking eastern branch of the
Roman Empire. "Numerous healing accounts are recounted throughout the writings
of Symeon the New Theologian (949–1022), Athanasius of Constantinople (1230–
1310), and Gregory Palamas (1296–1359)."

* Meesaeng Lee Choi, "Healing," *Encyclopedia of Christianity in the United
States*, Volume 3, ed. George Thomas Kurian and Mark A. Lamport (Lanham,
Maryland: Rowman & Littlefield, 2016), 1063.

Although outright rejections would never be uttered, more and more questioned the active role of the supernatural.

Reflecting on 1 Corinthians 12:1–2, John Chrysostom (347–407) expressed skepticism about healing and the gifts of the Spirit. In one homily, he proclaimed the following:

> This whole place is very obscure: but the obscurity is produced by our ignorance of the facts referred to and by their cessation, being such as then used to occur but now no longer take place. And why do they not happen now? Why look now, the cause too of the obscurity hath produced us again another question: namely, why did they then happen, and now do so no more?[3]

Chrysostom was not alone. An anonymous biblical commentator known as Ambrosiaster also demonstrated cessationist tendencies. Contemplating healing and spiritual gifts in his 1 Corinthians commentary, Ambrosiaster writes

> Why is it that people today do not have the grace of God in this way? These things had to happen at the beginning in order to give the faith a sure foundation. But now it is not necessary because people are bringing each other to the faith when

---

3. John Chrysostom, "Homily 29, First Corinthians 12:1–2," *A Select Library of Nicene and Post-Nicene Fathers of the Christian Church*, Volume 12, ed. Phillip Schaff (New York: Charles Scribner's Sons, 1889), 168.

they see good works and hear straightforward
preaching.[4]

Ambrosiaster suggests the healing and miraculous works
were needed in the early years of the church to provide a
durable foundation, but once the church was established, such
manifestations were no longer necessary. Ethical behavior and
"straightforward preaching" were enough to move things
forward.

In a similar way, the insights of Theodoret of Cyrus (393–
466) are observed. After residing in a monastery for seven years,
he was elected bishop of Cyrus and became an influential
theologian. Included in his duties as bishop, Theodoret
oversaw several monasteries and hermitages. He shouldered the
responsibility of protecting them from false doctrine and the
influences of the pagans.

Theodoret felt compelled to elaborate on why healing and
spiritual gifts were not as prominent as they were during the
era of the original apostles. Interacting with 1 Corinthians
12:1–2, he wrote the following:

> In former times those who accepted the divine
> preaching and who were baptized for their
> salvation were given visible signs of the grace of the

---

4. Ambrosiaster, "Commentary on 1 Corinthians 12:31," *Commentary on
Romans and 1–2 Corinthians*, trans. Gerald Bray (Downer's Drove, Illinois: Intervarsity
Press, 2009), 182.

> Holy Spirit at work in them . . . Even in our time
> grace is given to those who are deemed worthy of
> holy baptism, but it may not take the same form as
> it did in those days.[5]

Theodoret is suggesting that baptism, at one time, enabled the release of healing and other spiritual gifts, but its function had been reconfigured. Those being baptized now were encountering other kinds of gifts. This perspective illustrates an emerging cessationist ethos.

Gifts Taken Away?

By the seventh century, Gregory the Great (540–604), a prominent early pope, inched away from the miraculous and espoused a restrained form of cessationism. Gregory did not completely dismiss spiritual gifts. [6] Nevertheless, he sided with

---

5. Theodoret of Cyrus, 1 Corinthians 12:1, 7, *Commentary on the First Epistle to the Corinthians*, referenced by John MacArthur, *Strange Fire: The Danger of Offending the Holy Spirit With Counterfeit Worship* (Nashville: Thomas Nelson, 2013), 253.

6. Gregory was convinced that "miracles were necessary in the early church to accomplish the work of evangelism." He also believed that the gifts of the Spirit enabled the "conversion of pagans." He knew that miracles were propelling the evangelization of the Anglo-Saxons. Gregory once recounted one of his own healing experiences: Severe pain was ravaging his body due to an intestinal illness. "In his distress, he asked the abbot Eleutherius of Spoleto to pray on his behalf. The prayer was no sooner said than he found strength returning to his weakened body, and his anxiety vanished." Stanley M. Burgess, "Proclaiming the Gospel with Miraculous Gifts in the Postbiblical Early Church," in *The Kingdom and the Power: Are Healing and the Spiritual Gifts Used by Jesus in the Early Church Meant for the Church Today?*, ed. Gary S. Greig, Kevin Springer (Ventura, California: Regal, 1993), 284, 285. Jerome, on one

Augustine and others who suggested that they were progressively removed from the church. He believed that miracles provided excellent scaffolding, but should be dismantled once the edifice was constructed.

Gregory suggested that healing and miracles were initially given so "that faith might grow; it had to be nourished by miracles; for we, too, when we plant shrubs, pour water on them till we see that they have [taken] a strong hold on the ground."[7] However, once the roots are firm, "we stop the watering."[8]

Due to his ascetic background, Gregory was more concerned with moral virtue than miracles. He pens

> There is no reason what we have said about the virtues should not also be said of those gifts of the Holy Spirit that declare virtue to the world. To some is given prophecy, to some speaking in tongues, while to others the power to heal. But those gifts are not always present in the mind the same way; it is clear that they are sometimes taken

occasion, points out that "signs and wonders," were "performed" by Gregory "to the great glory of the churches." Jerome, "Lives of Illustrious Men," 65, *Nicene and Post Nicene Fathers*, 2nd Series, Volume 3, ed. Phillip Schaff and Henry Wace New York: Christian Literature Company, 1890), 376.

7. Gregory The Great quoted in Jon Ruthven, *On the Cessation of the Charismata: The Protestant Polemic on Postbiblical Miracles* (Sheffield, England: Sheffield Academic Press, 1993, 1997), 31.

8. Ibid.

away for our benefit, lest the mind should swell with presumption.[9]

Gregory's understanding of spiritual gifts, based on Isaiah 11:1–2, pulled believers out of the supernatural ethos of 1 Corinthians 12. Drawing upon this Old Testament text, he emphasized moral virtue. Willingly de-emphasizing healing, prophecy, and other works, Gregory suggested that the gifts of the Spirit were wisdom, science, understanding, counsel, fortitude, piety, and the fear of the Lord.

Reflecting on this emphasis on spiritual gifts, Gregory asserted

> When wisdom, understanding, counsel, fortitude, knowledge, piety, and fear of the Lord are born in us through the coming of the Spirit (adventum spiritus), it is as though the offspring to come [i.e. the heavenly life] is born in our minds.[10]

Gregory was beloved by the masses and sincerely desired good to be expressed in the church. His yearning for righteousness and virtue in an increasingly corrupt religious

---

9. Gregory the Great, *Moralia in Job*, Books 1–5 and conclusion, 2.56.89, trans. James O'Donnell. http://www.georgetown.edu/faculty/jod/gregory.html (accessed March 12, 2016).

10. Gregory the Great, *Moralia in Job*, 1.27.28, trans. Thomas L. Humphries Jr. *Ascetic Pneumatology from John Cassian to Gregory the Great* (New York: Oxford University Press, 2013), 167.

system was noble. Yet, he inadvertently caused people to turn away from healing and the deeper works of the Spirit.

CHAPTER NINE

The Latin Vulgate and the Rise of Extreme Unction

Another factor hindering the understanding and practice of healing was the emergence of the Latin Vulgate in 405. This was a translation of the Bible formulated by Jerome (340–420), a prominent theologian and historian.

Along with other developments, Jerome redefined the meaning of James 5:14–15. When properly translated, the original Greek rendering declares

> Is anyone among you sick? Let them call the elders
> of the church to pray over them and anoint them
> with oil in the name of the Lord. And the prayer
> offered in faith will make the sick person well; the
> Lord will raise him up.

The phrase "make the sick person well" comes from a Greek term that means "heal." However, instead of a literal rendering, Jerome translated it as "save." This unfortunate choice redefined the text's meaning. Lawrence Althouse points out

> In translating the scriptures into the Latin Vulgate, St. Jerome's skepticism was probably instrumental in leading him to use the rather limited and technical Latin term *salvo*, later to be translated into English as "salvation," thereby changing the original healing-saving concept to a more limited one of salvation of the spirit or soul.[1]

This interpretation had ramifications for how the ministry of healing would be understood and practiced in Roman Catholicism. Through it, the sacrament of healing would be completely reconfigured. Morton Kelsey declared

> With the emphasis on the next life, a profound change took place in the sacrament of healing. Its meaning shifted to the healing of soul in preparation. Unction for healing became unction for dying.[2]

---

1. Lawrence W. Althouse, "Healing and Health in the Judaic-Christian Experience: A Return to Holism," *Journal of Holistic Nursing* 3:1 (Spring 1985), 21.

2. Morton Kelsey, *Healing and Christianity: In Ancient Thought and Modern Times* (San Francisco, California: Harper and Row, 1973), 203.

What was once known as the sacrament of healing was, through Jerome's stimulus, redefined as "extreme unction"—a ceremonial rite for the dying. Francis MacNutt explains this tragic shift:

> As the attitude toward sickness changed and sickness became regarded more as a blessing than a curse, the purpose of the sacrament shifted until its primary effect was seen as spiritual: to prepare a soul in danger of death for immediate entrance into glory. Physical healing was still prominently mentioned in the words of the sacrament, but this was now regarded as its secondary purpose while its primary effect had to do with the soul. Its name became extreme unction. Originally this name, last anointing, only referred to the fact that it was the last in the list of seven sacraments with oil as part of its ritual. Later, in popular understanding, "last" came to mean the last act the church performed to prepare a person for death.[3]

Through the Latin Vulgate translation and changing ecclesiastical transitions, the sacrament of the healing transformed into preparation for death. Reflecting on what transpired, Philip Clayton states

---

3. Francis MacNutt, *Healing* (Notre Dame, Indiana: Ava Maria Press, 1974), 49–50.

Those involved in the ritual apparently ceased to expect that healing would result, focusing instead on the need for forgiveness of sin and an individual's preparation for death and the life to come. Gradually, healing came to be seen as a "conditional and occasional effect" of extreme unction, a rare by-product of the practice rather than its primary goal.[4]

In the aftermath of these transitions, the bishops, priests, and officers of the church were less likely to pray for the sick. Nevertheless, this reconfiguration did not change the fact that the masses still clamored for physical deliverance.

---

4. Phillip Clayton, "Theology of Spiritual Healing," in *Spiritual Healing: Scientific and Religious Perspectives*, ed. Fraser Watts (New York: Cambridge University Press, 2011), 47–48.

CHAPTER TEN

Healing's "Materiality"

Medieval Christians had "a binary understanding of the cosmos: God is Spirit, and he had created a material world, ontologically related to him, but metaphysically different."[1] It was the church's role to be a bridge between these worlds "through rituals and symbols."[2] This world "pulsated with accessibility to the divine, replete as it was with material points of contact with the spiritual realm."[3]

The spiritual sons and daughters of Rome "had a way of interweaving metaphysical strands."[4] In their minds, much of

---

1. Carlos Eire, "Redefining the Sacred and the Supernatural: How Protestant Reformation Really Did Disenchant the World," *Protestantism After 500 Years*, ed. Thomas Albert Howard and Mark A. Noll (Oxford University Press, 2016), 78.

2. Ibid.

3. Ibid.

4. Ibid, 92.

the tangible world throbbed "with the miraculous, or at least with the expectation of miracles."[5] Thus, healing was increasingly "mediated by physical objects."[6] Not only through consecrated oil or Eucharistic elements but also through other forms of "materiality."

The monastics "who reached the pinnacle of holiness were considered living proof of the divinization of matter."[7] In addition to their hands or feet, their clothing and personal effects also imbibed the reality of the supernatural.

An example of a monk's belongings conveying healing is witnessed by Martin of Tours (336–397), a former Roman soldier who became a bishop. Sulpicius Severus (363–420) recounts how

> threads from Martin's garment, or such as had been plucked from the sackcloth, which he wore,

---

5. Ibid.

6. Michael J. McClymond, "Charismatic Gifts: Healing, Tongue-Speaking, Prophecy, and Exorcism," in *The Wiley-Blackwell Companion to World Christianity*, ed. Lamin Sanneh and Michael J. McClymond (West Sussex, United Kingdom: John Wiley and Sons, 2016), 405.

7. Carlos Eire, "Redefining the Sacred and the Supernatural: How Protestant Reformation Really Did Disenchant the World," *Protestantism After 500 Years*, ed. Thomas Albert Howard and Mark A. Noll (Oxford University Press, 2016), 83. "They not only conversed with Christ and the Virgin Mary but also had ineffable encounters with the Godhead; they swooned in rapture, went into trances, levitated, bilocated, read minds, prophesied, manifested the wounds of Christ on their bodies, and healed the sick and lame. Once they died, their corpses could admit a wonderful aroma and remain intact."

wrought frequent miracles upon those who were sick. For, by either being tied round the fingers or placed about the neck, they very often drove away diseases from the afflicted.[8]

Severus also relates how a letter from Martin of Tours was actively utilized to petition healing from God.

Arborius, an ex-prefect, and a man of a very holy and faithful character, while his daughter was in agony from the burning fever of a quartan ague, inserted in the bosom of the girl, at the very paroxysm of the heat, a letter of Martin which happened to have been brought to him, and immediately the fever was dispelled.[9]

A similar outworking is demonstrated through the life of Cuthbert (634–687). One of his contemporaries declared, "The very garments which had been on St. Cuthbert's body, either while living or after he was dead, were not exempt from the virtue of performing cures."[10]

---

8. Sulpicius Severus, "On the Life of Martin, 18," *Nicene and Post-Nicene Fathers of the Christian Church*, Second Series, Volume 11, trans. Phillip Schaff and Henry Wace (New York: Christian Literature Crusade, 1894), 12.

9. Sulpicius Severus, "On the Life of Martin, 19," *Nicene and Post-Nicene Fathers of the Christian Church*, Second Series, Volume 11, trans. Phillip Schaff and Henry Wace (New York: Christian Literature Crusade, 1894), 13.

10. Bede, *Venerable Bede's Ecclesiastical History of England*, 4:31, ed. J. A. Giles (London: Henry G. Bohn, 1849), 234.

In one instance, a young man suffering from paralysis in his feet was healed when they took the shoes off of Cuthbert's deceased body and placed them on the young man. Bede writes

> And as the virtue of healing that was bestowed through the relics of the holy man advanced, the soundness that he had prayed for continued to pass from the soles of his feet through the rest of his limbs.[11]

---

11. Bede, "Life and Miracles of Saint Cuthbert," 45, Bishop of Lindisfarne in *Complete Works of Venerable Bede*, Volume 4, ed. J. A. Giles (London: Whittaker and Co, 1943), 351.

CHAPTER ELEVEN

Relics

Ecclesiastical officials made it clear that the channel for "divine power was through the saints."[1] Only individuals with an obvious sanctity could broker healing. Non-clergy were often discouraged from interacting with the sick or uttering spontaneous prayers "tailored to the sick person's need." The laity were forbidden to participate in "the laying on of hands," and from suggesting that healing "might be transmitted by the human touch."[2]

Those who desired healing were forced to travel to hermitages and monasteries. If one were unable to access a notable intercessor, prayer "might be done by a priest of less

---

1. Meredith B. McGuire, *Lived Religion: Faith and Practice in Everyday Life* (New York: Oxford University Press 2008), 37–38.

2. Francis MacNutt, *Healing Reawakening*, (Grand Rapids: Chosen Books, 2005), 111, 130.

pronounced personality and reputation."[3] For most Christians, this option was unacceptable. They naturally wanted those whose prayers were efficacious.

The truly desperate were willing to locate sanctity anywhere—even among the effects of the deceased. Catholics believed that the ontology of holiness could permeate environments and physical objects. So something directly associated with a saint was thought to have a similar nature. Thus healing virtue could permeate buildings, sacramental objects, books, or personal belongings. Accessing a "sanctified object" not only activated faith, but it also mediated supernatural power. Michael McClymond points out

> By the high Middle Ages . . . there were fewer reported healings from the prayers of living saints and more resulting from the purported effects of physical objects associated with saints. Bones, teeth, hair, body parts, burial sites, and other "relics" associated with the saints reputedly brought healing to the sick.[4]

---

3. Wilfred Bonser, *The Medical Background of Anglo-Saxon England* (United Kingdom: Oxford University Press, 1963), 173.

4. Michael J. McClymond, "Charismatic Gifts: Healing, Tongue-Speaking, Prophecy, and Exorcism," in *The Wiley-Blackwell Companion to World Christianity*, ed. Lamin Sanneh and Michael J. McClymond (West Sussex, United Kingdom: John Wiley and Sons, 2016), 405.

The faithful believed that they could be healed through a relic, an "object, notably part of the body or clothes, remaining as a memorial of a departed saint."[5] This included any number of things, including the "remains of saints' bodies, objects used by saints (e.g., clothing), or anything that had touched saints' remains or even their tombs."[6]

Articulating a fourth-century understanding of relics, Jerome (347–420) writes

> We do not worship, we do not adore, for fear that
> we should bow down to the creature rather than to
> the Creator, but we venerate the relics of the
> martyrs in order the better to adore him whose
> martyrs they are.[7]

Conveying a similar ethos, Herbert Thurton references the following conception of relics:

> The classical instance is to be found in the letter
> written by the inhabitants of Smyrna, about 156,
> describing the death of St. Polycarp. After he had

---

5. Herbert Thurston, "Relics," *Catholic Encyclopedia*, ed. Charles G. Herbermann, Edward Pace, Conde Pallen, Thomas Shahan, and John Wynne (New York: Robert Appleton Company, 1914), 22.

6. Ronald Kydd, "Healing in the Christian Church," *The New International Dictionary of Pentecostal and Charismatic Movements,* ed. Stanley M. Burgess and Eduard M. van der Maas (Grand Rapids: Zondervan, 2002), 698–711.

7. Jerome, *Ad Riparium,* i, P.L., XXII, 907, referenced in Thomas J. Craughwell, *Saints Preserved: An Encyclopedia of Relics* (New York: Image Books, 2011), xiii.

been burnt at the stake, we are told that his faithful disciples wished to carry off his remains, but the Jews urged the Roman officer to refuse his consent for fear that the Christians "would only abandon the Crucified One and begin to worship this man." Eventually, however, as the Smyrnaeans say, "We took up his bones, which are more valuable than precious stones and finer than refined gold, and laid them in a suitable place, where the Lord will permit us to gather ourselves together, as we are able, in gladness and joy, and to celebrate the birthday of his martyrdom." This is the keynote which is echoed in a multitude of similar passages found a little later in the patristic writers of both East and West.[8]

In affirming the viability of relics, some drew upon 2 Kings 13:21 from the Old Testament. It recounts the resuscitation of a dead man after touching Elisha's bones. Elsewhere it was pointed out that the glory of God could be transmitted through the fibers of a minister's clothing. Ezekiel pens

When the priests return to the outer courtyard where the people are, they must take off the clothes they wear while ministering to me. They must leave

---

8. Herbert Thurston, "Relics," *Catholic Encyclopedia*, ed. Charles G. Herbermann, Edward Pace, Conde Pallen, Thomas Shahan, and John Wynne (New York: Robert Appleton Company, 1914), 22.

them in the sacred rooms and put on other clothes, so they do not endanger anyone by transmitting holiness to them through this clothing" (Ezekiel 44:18–19 NLT).

A few other biblical passages also imply that the transference of power could take place through physical contact (See Luke 8:46, Acts 5:15, 19:12). Many were convinced that these verses gave credence to the efficacy of relics.

Though relics were older artifacts, in the minds of the faithful, they brought "deliverance and pardon into the present."[9] The glory and fervor of previous eras could be directly encountered in succeeding generations.

The Dust of the Dead

Though once a great skeptic, Augustine (354–430) witnessed miracles and subsequently changed his outlook. He publicly acknowledged that healings had taken place through relics housed in his church. He wrote

> I realized how many miracles were occurring in our own day and which were so like the miracles of old and also how wrong it would be to allow the memory of these marvels of divine power to perish from among our people. It is only two years ago

---

9. Ronald Kydd, *Healing Through the Centuries* (Peabody, Massachusetts: Hendrickson, 1998), 121.

that the keeping of records was begun here in Hippo, and already, at this writing, we have nearly seventy attested miracles.[10]

The following is an account of physical rejuvenation written by Augustine that took place during his oversight:

The miracle which was wrought at Milan when I was there, and by which a blind man was restored to sight, could come to the knowledge of many; for not only is the city a large one but also the emperor was there at the time, and the occurrence was witnessed by an immense concourse of people who had gathered to the bodies of the martyrs Protasius and Gervasius, which had long lain concealed and unknown but were now made known to the bishop Ambrose in a dream and discovered by him. By virtue of these remains, the darkness of that blind man was scattered, and he saw the light of day.[11]

After witnessing this amazing occurrence, Augustine was elated. He boldly declared

Praise to God was shouted so loudly that my ears could hardly stand the din. But, of course, the main

---

10. Augustine, *City of God*, in *Nicene and Post-Nicene Fathers*, First Series, Volume 2, trans. Marcus Dods (New York: The Christian Literature Company, 1886) 1954, 22.8.

11. Ibid.

point was that, in the hearts of all this clamoring crowd, there burned that faith in Christ.[12]

In a homily, Augustine once referenced the viability of relics, saying that God "grants us such favors from the dust of the dead."[13]

Is This Not Like What We've Read in the Gospels?

Ambrose (340–397), bishop of Milan, recounting stories of reliquary healing, was "struck by the similarity between the miraculous which characterized the church of his time and what he knew of events that took place during Jesus' life."[14]

In a letter to his sister, he described the discovery of the relics of Gervase and Protase. He noted, "We found two men of marvelous stature, such as those of ancient days. All the bones were perfect, and there was much blood."[15] Jefferson records, "Following the unearthing of the holy remains as if to

---

12. Augustine, *The City of God*, trans. William Babcock, notes by Boniface Ramsey (Hyde Park, New York: New City Press, 2012), 450.

13. Augustine, "Sermon 317.1," in Augustine of Hippo, *Sermons (306–340A) on the Saints*, trans. Edmund Hill (Hyde Park, New York: New City Press, 1994), 1435.

14. Ronald Kydd, "Jesus, Saints, and Relics: Approaching the Early Church Through Healing," *Journal of Pentecostal Theology* 1.2 (1993), 97.

15. Ambrose, "Letter 22," Letters of Saint Ambrose, *Nicene and Post-Nicene Fathers*, Second Series, Volume 10, ed. Philip Schaff and Henry Wace (Buffalo: Christian Literature Publishing Co., 1896), 437.

legitimate the discovery, a blind man's sight was restored."[16] Reflecting on this, Ambrose writes

> You have heard, nay, yourselves have seen, many cleansed from evil spirits; many also, after touching with their hands the garments of the saints, delivered from the infirmities under which they suffered: you have seen the miracles of old time renewed, when through the coming of the Lord Jesus, a fuller grace descended upon the earth; you see many healed by the shadow, as it were, of the holy bodies. How many napkins are passed to and fro? How many garments placed on these holy relics, and endowed by the mere contact with the power of healing are reclaimed by their owners. All think themselves happy in touching even the outermost thread, and whoever touches them will be made whole.[17]

Ambrose was also defending the veracity of the relics, insisting that the blind man had, in fact, been cured. He explained that the man had personally testified to his healing: "He declares that when he touched the border of the garment with which the martyrs' bodies were clothed, his sight was

---

16. Lee M. Jefferson, *Christ Miracle Worker in Early Christian Art* (Minneapolis, Minnesota: Fortress Press 2014), 80.

17. Ambrose, "Letter 22," in *The Letters of Saint Ambrose Bishop of Milan with Notes and Indices* (London: James Parker and Company, 1881), 160.

restored to him." [18] Ambrose then inquires, "Is not this like what we read in the gospel? For the power which we admire proceeds from one and the same Author."[19]

The Invasion of the Mundane

The healings made a considerable impact. Frend notes that "the effect on the Arian population and Empress Justina was considerable."[20] Justina (340–388) was the second wife of Valentinian I (reigned 364–375) and the mother of Valentinian II (reigned 375–392). Although she did not turn "to the soundness of believing," because of the remarkable reports, Justina "turned back from her fury of persecuting."[21]

Similar experiences were recounted. Some years later, Abbess Aelfleda of Whitby, England, was so weak in body that she could not stand. As she lay in bed, she remembered Cuthbert, a gifted monk and close friend. She said, "I would that I had something belonging to my dear Cuthbert, for I

---

18. Ibid., 163.

19. Ibid.

20. W. H. C. Frend, "The Place of Miracles in the Conversion of the Ancient World to Christianity," in *Signs, Wonders, Miracles: Representations of Divine Power in the Life of the Church*, ed. Kate Cooper and Jeremy Gregory (Rochester: Boydell and Brewer, 2005), 17.

21. Augustine, "Confessions," in *A Library of Fathers of the Holy Catholic Church*, Volume 1, trans. E. B. Pusey (London: Oxford, 1840), 168.

know of a surety, and I trust in the Lord, that I soon should be healed." [22] Bede mentions

> Not long after, there arrived one who brought with him a linen girdle, which Cuthbert had sent to her . . . She girt it around her, and the next morning she was able to stand erect, and on the third day, she was restored to perfect health. [23]

There were other remarkable testimonies along these same lines. Ronald Finucane, in his groundbreaking work on relics, recounted the following story:

> A man crippled by birth got about by dragging himself along with hand-trestles. His thumb, too, was bent back, the nail nearly through the palm. While huddled at Godric's tomb, crying and moaning, he straightened his legs and began to extend them. During this, many heard a crackling noise of bones and ligaments stretching. At dawn, he arose and walked up to present the trestles as an

---

22. Abbess Aelfleda of Whitby quoted in Bede, "Life and Miracles of Saint Cuthbert, Bishop of Lindisfarne," in *Complete Works of Venerable Bede*, Volume 4, ed. J. A. Giles (London: Whittaker and Co., 1943), 283, 285.

23. Bede, *Life and Miracles of Saint Cuthbert, Bishop of Lindisfarne*, in *Complete Works of Venerable Bede*, Volume 4, ed. J. A. Giles (London: Whittaker and Co, 1943), 283, 285.

offering; his hand was healed, only a red spot remaining on his palm.[24]

In 633, Bishop Cummian (591–662) attempted to persuade reluctant Irish leaders to accept the efficacy of relics. In coaxing them, he asserted

> We have proofs of the virtue of God being in the relics of the holy martyrs, and in the writings which they have brought hither. With our own eyes, we have seen a totally blind girl open her eyes before these relics, and we have seen a lame man walk.[25]

Similar occurrences gripped the hearts of the masses, sparking faith. He is not just the God of mysticism and wonder; He is also the God who is willing to invade the mundane of human existence.

Keener writes, "Strange as it appears to many readers today, though, church fathers like Basil, Chrysostom, Ambrose, and Augustine believed that the healing often was mediated through relics."[26]

---

24. Ronald C. Finucane, *Miracles and Pilgrims: Popular Beliefs in Medieval England* (London: J. M. Dent and Sons Ltd, 1977), 91.

25. Cummian quoted in Heinrich Zimmer, *The Celtic Church in Britain and Ireland*, trans. A. Meyer (London: Nutt, 1902), 123.

26. Craig S. Keener, *Miracles: The Credibility of the New Testament Accounts* (Grand Rapids: Baker, 2011), 363. Ramsey MacMullen, *Second Church, Popular Christianity AD 200–400* (Atlanta: Society of Biblical Literature, 2009), 65, 90, 108.

CHAPTER TWELVE

Shrines and Pilgrimages

Within the medieval ethos, it was not relics alone but also encounters at particular locales that captured the imagination. Often, sanctuaries and large edifices "were built around martyrs' graves in the cemeteries and became centers of pilgrimage."[1] In the modern vernacular, these "shrines were faith-healing centers."[2]

---

1. Andrew Daunton-Fear, *Healing in the Early Church: The Church's Ministry of Healing and Exorcism from the First to the Fifth Century* (Eugene, Oregon: Wipf & Stock, 2009), 143. If one were to visit the shrines, he or she would find "wretched cripples writhing on the floor . . . screams of unfettered madmen straining at their bonds and the low moans of lepers and the blind, and by the characteristic odor of the Middle Ages, the stench of poverty and disease." Ronald C. Finucane, *Miracles and Pilgrims: Popular Beliefs in Medieval England* (New York: St. Martin's Press, 1977, 1995), 10.

2. Ronald C. Finucane, *Miracles and Pilgrims: Popular Beliefs in Medieval England* (New York: St. Martin's Press, 1977, 1995), 67.

For the faithful, it was as if the very dirt that the memorials rested upon were imbibed with power from on high. Finucane recounts the story of a man named Henry who was healed as he applied some of the "dust" from the tomb of a saint. Finucane states

> Henry, paralyzed on the right side and carrying his arm in a sling, came to Simon de Montfort's tomb and took dust from it, which he rubbed on his arm. He was healed at once, before many witnesses.[3]

Around the ancient bones and paraphernalia, there were remarkable occurrences. One finds a number of testimonies of "cured blindness, deafness, speech disorders, and various conditions impairing a person's mobility."[4] What was most commonly restored were the

> various mobility impairments, while approximately one-third of recorded cures were healings of blinding conditions. Deafness and muteness, on the other hand, are much rarer.[5]

---

3. Ibid., 89.

4. Jenni Kuuliala, "Heavenly Healing or Failure of Faith? Partial Cures in Later Medieval Canonization," in *Processes, Church and Belief in the Middle Ages: Popes, Saints, and Crusaders,* ed. Kirsi Salonen and Sari Katajala-Peltomaa (Amsterdam, Netherlands: Amsterdam University Press, 2016), 171.

5. Ibid.

Recounting what was transpiring in one of the shrines, the English historian Roger de Wendover states

> miracles continue to be wrought at that spot; for, in the sight of numbers of witnesses, the deaf there recover their hearing, the lame walk, the blind see, and all who in faith invoke the aid of the blessed martyr, obtain of God the wished-for blessing, whether of mind or of body.[6]

Abbot Aelfric of Eynsham (955–1010) talked about a place of pilgrimage that "was hung round with crutches, and with the stools of cripples who had been healed, from one end to the other on either wall, and not even so could they put half of them up."[7] Documenting events at another shrine, Aelfric records

> Within ten days, two hundred men were healed and so many within twelve months that no man could count them. The burial ground lay filled with crippled folk, so that people could hardly get in to minister; and they were all so miraculously healed

6. Roger of Wendover, *Roger of Wendover Comprising the History of England from the Descent of the Saxons to AD 1235*, trans. J. A. Giles (London: Henry G. Bohn, 1849), 161. Roger draws his observation from the writings of Bede.

7. Aelfric, *Lives of Saints*, Volume 2, ed. Walter Skeat (London: N. Trübner & Company, 1881), 431–434.

within a few days that one could not find there five
unsound men out of that great crowd.[8]

Examining the records of the shrines in England,
Finucane was able to document astounding healings. In a crypt
in Canterbury Cathedral, "a deaf woman felt twigs snapping in
her head; while she screamed from the pain, a great deal of
bloody matter flowed from her ears, after which she could
hear."[9]

On another occasion, "a crippled Lincoln boy, with one
leg shorter than the other, went to St. Frideswide's Church.
There he was cured while his sinews were heard to crackle, and
both legs became equal."[10]

While some were immediately healed as they entered the
shrines, "a large proportion of the recoveries . . . were
gradual."[11] According to extant records, the vast majority "only
gradually became aware of an improvement in their health."[12]

---

8. Aelfric, *Aelfric's Lives of Saints,* Volume 1, ed. Walter Skeat (London: N.
Trübner & Company, 1881), 451.

9. Ronald C. Finucane, *Miracles and Pilgrims: Popular Beliefs in Medieval
England* (New York: St. Martin's Press, 1977, 1995), 89.

10. Ibid., 91.

11. Jenni Kuuliala, "Heavenly Healing or Failure of Faith? Partial Cures in Later
Medieval Canonization," in *Processes, Church and Belief in the Middle Ages: Popes, Saints,
and Crusaders,* ed. Kirsi Salonen and Sari Katajala-Peltomaa (Amsterdam,
Netherlands: Amsterdam University Press, 2016), 172.

12. Ronald C. Finucane, *Miracles and Pilgrims: Popular Beliefs in Medieval
England* (New York: St. Martin's Press, 1977, 1995), 69–70.

In most cases, the healing took weeks or months.[13] Finucane suggests

> most medieval miracles were not sudden, and if we expected to find as a daily occurrence cripples flinging away their crutches or mute pilgrims breaking out in a Te Deum, we would be disappointed. Certainly, a few cures were sudden, taking place as soon as the supplicant approached the holy dead, but these were not typical.[14]

In one instance, a blind woman went to Gilbert of Sempringham's tomb, prayed, and left still not able to see. However, in the days that followed, she incrementally improved "until her sight was restored."[15] On another occasion

> a mute girl waited with her mother for four or five days at Frideswide's shrine, but nothing happened, and at last the mother, bored with waiting, made ready to go home—with the theologically correct, but in this case, not a very comforting observation that God's power was the same everywhere. At this

---

13. Ibid., 76. Finucane writes, "Occasionally . . . this came easily, as it did for the cripple taken to Canterbury who knelt in prayer, arose, and relinquished her crutches. Most sick pilgrims, however, stood, knelt, sat, or slept in the church, waiting for something to happen." Ronald C. Finucane, *Miracles and Pilgrims: Popular Beliefs in Medieval England,* 76, 87.

14. Ibid., 75–76.

15. Ibid., 76.

the girl collapsed, slept, and on waking up began to speak.[16]

If a healing were not aptly received at a particular shrine, "a patient might be carried to others in turn. William of Malmesbury tells of a blind man who visited eighty-seven shrines while seeking a remedy."[17]

Apparently, there was a priest "who was paralyzed while singing mass. He visited shrines for the next three years, begging for health from the saints . . . until at last he was cured at Worcester, some sixty miles from his home."[18]

When possible, the afflicted would incubate, which was the practice of sleeping in the crypts. After staying the night at Cantilupe's shrine, a cripple, "[at] about sunrise, was seen to stand up and walk."[19] A blind girl from Eynsham who desired healing was "taken to the shrine [where] she slept at the

---

16. Ibid., 77–78.

17. Wilfred Bonser, *The Medical Background of Anglo-Saxon England* (United Kingdom: Oxford University Press, 1963), 181–182.

18. Ronald C. Finucane, *Miracles and Pilgrims: Popular Beliefs in Medieval England* (New York: St. Martin's Press, 1977, 1995), 85. Earlier in the book, Finucane writes, "Physical as well as verbal evidence was offered, as in the case of the man who came before the pope claiming to have been cured of leprosy . . . He had to remove his shirt to prove that he was of a uniform color, which was supposed to allay any suspicions of cosmetic treatment of his skin." Ronald C. Finucane, *Miracles and Pilgrims: Popular Beliefs in Medieval England* (New York: St. Martin's Press, 1977, 1995), 54.

19. Ibid., 89.

sepulcher. In the morning, after shedding many tears, bloody pus flowed from her eyes, and she recovered her sight."[20]

When an infirmed man or woman made healing claims, the keepers of the shrine sought corroboration, asking him or her to perform exercises or complete a basic test. Finucane points out

> Those who had once been blind identified things: an egg or a coin, or named colors, or followed lighted candles. Cripples were asked to walk about: after screaming, twisting and moaning in the Canterbury crypt, a sixteen-year-old girl breathlessly announced her cure, but, just to make certain, the monks made her pace up and down. One cured woman overcame the registrar's doubts by obligingly lying down and getting up from the ground with great agility.[21]

When possible, the keepers of the shrines would also interview witnesses who had first-hand knowledge of the men or women claiming to have been healed.

> They wanted to know, for example, how the witness had come to learn of the miracle; what words were used by those who had prayed for the miracle; and whether any herbs, stones, other

---

20. Ibid.
21. Ibid., 101.

> natural or medicinal preparations or incantations had accompanied the miracle . . . Of course, witnesses were also asked in what year, month, day, place, and in whose presence the wonderful event itself occurred.[22]

Verified reports were immediately spread far and wide, inspiring others to seek physical deliverance at the named shrines. There is little doubt that as "healing began to appear less and less in the church's ritual, it began to appear more and more at shrines, pilgrimage sites, and in connection with holy relics."[23]

---

22. Ibid., 53.

23. Lawrence W. Althouse, "Healing and Health in the Judaic-Christian Experience: A Return to Holism," *Journal of Holistic Nursing* 3:1 (Spring 1985), 22.

CHAPTER THIRTEEN

Reliquary Healing and the Westward Expansion

What is fascinating is that reliquarial healing became "one of the most expedient of all missionary devices."[1] It became a catalyst for the expansion of Christianity into the pagan outlands. Darrel Amundsen remarked, "The cult of the saints and relics was the single most important force in the conversion of western Europe."[2] As the church expanded "during the early Middle Ages, the cult of the saints and relics was imported into the realm of the barbarians."[3]

---

1. Ronald C. Finucane, *Miracles and Pilgrims: Popular Beliefs in Medieval England* (New York: St. Martin's Press, 1977, 1995), 20.

2. Darrel Amundsen, *Medicine, Society and Faith in the Ancient and Medieval Worlds* (Baltimore: Johns Hopkins University Press, 1998), 181.

3. Ibid., 191.

Mosheim reiterated that "the conversions of the barbarous nations to Christianity must be ascribed principally to the prodigies and miracles that were wrought."[4] The Ostrogoths, Visigoths, and Vandals were introduced "to a religion impregnated with miracles and saintly wonders."[5] For a majority of those who were converted, "the bones of holy men and their relics became the very core of Christianity."[6]

It was said that the Anglo-Saxon missionary Boniface (672–754) brought many Germans in the Frankish Empire into the church through "sound doctrine and miracles."[7] In a similar way, Martin of Tours (336–397) "brought about conversions by preaching, healing and knocking down pagan shrines."[8] Pope Gregory I wrote to Augustine of Canterbury (570–604) in 601, commending him for the successful evangelization of the Anglo-Saxons. The pontiff believed that the English souls were "drawn by outward miracles to inward

4. John Laurence von Mosheim, *Institutes of Ecclesiastical History, Ancient and Modern*, Volume 1 (New York: Robert Cater & Brothers 1801), 358.

5. Ronald C. Finucane, *Miracles and Pilgrims: Popular Beliefs in Medieval England* (New York: St. Martin's Press, 1977, 1995), 20.

6. Darrel Amundsen, *Medicine, Society and Faith in the Ancient and Medieval Worlds* (Baltimore: Johns Hopkins University Press, 1998), 191.

7. F. R. Hoare, *The Western Fathers: Being the Lives of Martin of Tours, Ambrose, Augustine of Hippo, Honoratus of Arles, and Germanus of Auxerre* (London: Sheed and Ward, 1980), 307. C. H. Talbot, *The Anglo-Saxon Missionaries in Germany* (London: Sheed and Ward, 1954), 213.

8. Ronald C. Finucane, *Miracles and Pilgrims: Popular Beliefs in Medieval England* (New York: St. Martin's Press, 1977, 1995), 21.

grace."[9] These practices had grown so significant that "the Second Council of Nicaea held in 787 decreed that no church should be consecrated without relics."[10]

The miracles "recorded at English and Continental shrines from the twelfth through the fifteenth centuries involved healings and the alleviations of physical ills."[11] For several centuries

> the beliefs and miraculous practices associated with . . . relics dominated Western Christianity . . . For the physically ill or maimed, or the demon possessed, these shrines became a focal point for hope, comfort, healing, and social and spiritual reintegration throughout the Middle Ages . . . Although not the sole means of healing in the church's repertoire, the cult of saints and relics overshadowed all other sources of licit miraculous healing.[12]

---

9. Gregory quoted in Bede, *Ecclesiastical History* 1.31, trans. B. Colgrave and R. Mynors (Oxford, United Kingdom: Clarendon, 1969. "Augustine's missionary monks were admired for their exemplary way of life and delightful promises which, by many miracles, they proved to be most certain." Ronald C. Finucane, *Miracles and Pilgrims: Popular Beliefs in Medieval England* (New York: St. Martin's Press, 1977, 1995), 21.

10. Wilfred Bonser, *The Medical Background of Anglo-Saxon England* (United Kingdom: Oxford University Press, 1963), 181.

11. Darrel Amundsen, *Medicine, Society and Faith in the Ancient and Medieval Worlds* (Baltimore, Maryland: Johns Hopkins University Press, 1998), 181.

12. Ibid., 191.

Keener notes that "critics uncomfortable with power in the relics themselves, including many modern readers, might nevertheless allow that they sometimes served as a contact point for supplicants' faith in God."[13]

---

13. Craig S. Keener, *Miracles: The Credibility of the New Testament Accounts*, (Grand Rapids, Michigan: Baker, 2011), 370.

CHAPTER FOURTEEN

Superstition and Excess

Although authentic healings transpired, relics and shrines had for some become "a substitute for some of the pagan practices."[1] Segments had become fixated on amulets, magic, and other unsavory things. Ulrich Lehner suggests that if

> the touching of a relic lifted the mind up to contemplate the core mysteries of the faith, that could be useful. But if they are believed to be "powerful" in themselves, like charms, they had become vehicles of superstition.[2]

---

1. Darrel Amundsen, *Medicine, Society and Faith in the Ancient and Medieval Worlds* (Baltimore, Maryland: Johns Hopkins University Press, 1998), 191.

2. Ulrich L. Lehner, *The Catholic Enlightenment: The Forgotten History of a Global Movement* (New York: Oxford University Press, 2106), 131.

Herbert Thurton acknowledges that relics "easily lent themselves to error, fraud, and greed of gain."[3] This breakdown is evidenced through the pages of Geoffrey Chaucer's late medieval work *Canterbury Tales* (1478). In this collection of stories

> Chaucer's Pardoner carried bottles of pigs' bones and bits of rags which he claimed to be relics of great saints. He hypocritically told church audiences that those bones and rags would heal all their ailments as well as those of their animals.[4]

These growing misapplications did not sit well with many church leaders.[5] Ronald Kydd observed the following:

> Throughout the centuries, theologians struggled to shape the devotion to relics, but they met with little success. The dilemma they faced was how to endorse the sanctity of relics and the intervention of the saints, which enjoyed such popular acclaim,

---

3. Herbert Thurston, "Relics," *Catholic Encyclopedia*, ed. Charles G. Herbermann, Edward Pace, Conde Pallen, Thomas Shahan, and John Wynne (New York: Robert Appleton Company, 1914), 22.

4. William DeArteaga, *Quenching the Spirit: Discover the Real Spirit Behind the Charismatic Controversy* (Orlando, Florida: Creation House, 1996), 77.

5. Some were more concerned that the pilgrims "neglected hearth and home to endure months, even years of journeying in search of cures and the promise of grace at the continent's most prominent shrines." Philp M. Soergel, *Miracles and the Protestant Imagination: The Evangelical Wonder Book in Reformation Germany* (New York: Oxford University Press, 2012), 35.

without condoning attendant excesses, which could become extraordinarily bizarre.[6]

Wanting to encourage wonder, little was done to counteract excess. Narrating the usual Roman Catholic outlook, Robert Bruce Mullin affirmed

> in popular devotions such as reverencing the relics of some ancient saint, there was at best only a probability that the relics were derived from the saint in question. They might be spurious. Yet the church chose, nonetheless, to permit such devotions. Why? Precisely . . . because there was at least some probable evidence on their behalf. If the church could not be sure that the relics were genuine, it could not be sure that the relics were fraudulent. Furthermore, one could see that the faith of the believers was real, and the church had always maintained that it was better to err on the side of faith.[7]

The pope and church officials simply did not want the people to lose their sense of awe.

---

6. Ronald Kydd, *Healing in the Christian Church*, *The New International Dictionary of Pentecostal and Charismatic Movements*, ed. Stanley M. Burgess and Eduard M. van der Maas (Grand Rapids, Michigan: Zondervan, 2002), 698–711.

7. Robert Bruce Mullin, *Miracles and the Modern Religious Imagination* (New Haven, Connecticut: Yale University Press, 1997), 128.

Fraudulent Healings?

Although many critics would suggest that "it is impossible to accept the medieval accounts of organic diseases being permanently cured in this way,"[8] much of the extant evidence upholds its validity.

Finucane acknowledges that "no doubt fraud explains some of the recorded cases, but it is unlikely that the majority of them can be accounted for in this way."[9] Despite corruption, error, and misapplication, an inexplicable number of healings were reported as a result of pilgrimages and engagements with relics.[10]

Although modern researchers dispute the hagiographic[11] reports, what they assert "may well retain the substance of the

---

8. Wilfred Bonser, *The Medical Background of Anglo-Saxon England* (United Kingdom: Oxford University Press, 1963), 173.

9. Ronald C. Finucane, *Miracles and Pilgrims: Popular Beliefs in Medieval England* (New York: St. Martin's Press, 1977, 1995), 71.

10. Michael J. McClymond suggests that there are at least 3,000 miracle reports from French and English shrines in just the twelfth and thirteenth centuries. Michael J. McClymond, *Charismatic Gifts: Healing, Tongue-Speaking, Prophecy, and Exorcism*, in *The Wiley-Blackwell Companion to World Christianity*, ed. Lamin Sanneh and Michael J. McClymond (West Sussex, United Kingdom: John Wiley and Sons, 2016), 405.

11. Finucane writes, "Hagiographers busied themselves in extolling the wonderful penances and frightful austerities of their subjects, their charity, chastity and charisma . . . extreme piety, fears of healing, and so on. They did not produce what one could call an impartial biography—if such a thing has ever existed—but on the contrary they often went in for highly embellished accounts of the lives and miracles of their saints." Ronald C. Finucane, *Miracles and Pilgrims: Popular Beliefs in Medieval England* (New York: St. Martin's Press, 1977, 1995), 52.

events."[12] There is little doubt that those who lived during the Middle Ages "experienced miracles as real."[13] Reflecting on this, Meredith McGuire states

> One of the reasons we misinterpret medieval religious practice as merely "superstitious" or "irrational" is that we fail to grasp practitioners' conception of religious power. A mode of action is not irrational if a person perceives it to work. Given their conception of religious power, medieval persons were reasonable to consider ritual actions to be the appropriate and efficacious way to meet certain needs and to accomplish certain tasks. People experienced that power as real. These cultures socialized their members' very senses to perceive divine power. Thus, not only did they think about this religious power differently than do most twenty-first-century Europeans but also they had regular experiences in which they sensed it. Divine power was not just a matter of belief; it was an awesome and important reality in people's lives.[14]

---

12. Craig S. Keener, *Miracles: The Credibility of the New Testament Accounts* (Grand Rapids, Michigan: Baker, 2011), 369.

13. Meredith B. McGuire, *Lived Religion: Faith and Practice in Everyday Life* (New York: Oxford University Press, 2008), 34.

14. Ibid., 33.

Documentary evidence suggests that the "reliquarial approach to the miraculous dominated Christian thought and practice with regard to healing much longer than any others."[15] Beginning in late antiquity and continuing through the Middle Ages, "claims to healing associated with relics were common."[16]

---

15. Ronald Kydd, *Healing Through the Centuries* (Peabody, Massachusetts: Hendrickson, 1998), 117.

16. Ibid.

CHAPTER FIFTEEN

The Reconfiguration of Healing

Although the ministry of healing endured throughout the middle ages,[1] it became fundamentally reconfigured. In many ways, the validation of relics and their accouterments expose a "shifting ethos"[2] in the church.

---

1. Another significant movement was the Waldensians, which originated in Lyon, France, in 1173. It was started as an effort by Peter Waldo (1140–1218) to give away his wealth to help the poor. Others joined him, and there were reports of healings taking place. The Waldensio Confessio (1431) declared, "Therefore, concerning this anointing of the sick, we hold it as an article of faith, and profess sincerely from the heart that sick persons, when they ask it, may lawfully be anointed with the anointing oil by one who joins with them in praying that it may be efficacious to the healing of the body according to the design and end and effect mentioned by the apostles; and we profess that such an anointing, performed according to the apostolic design and practice, will be healing and profitable." The Catholic Church viewed the Waldensians as heretical. At the 1184 Synod of Verona, directed by Pope Lucius III and the Holy Roman Emperor Frederick I, they were excommunicated.

2. Ronald Kydd, "Jesus, Saints, and Relics: Approaching the Early Church Through Healing," Journal of Pentecostal Theology 1:2 (1993), 98.

Fundamentally, the "living practitioners had, to some extent, lost sight of the simplicity of the methods of the earlier age, and the dead could not encourage repentance and faith in Christ."[3] It is easy to get entangled in a changing world.

Over time, some of the healing practices became bizarre—indistinguishable from wives' tales and folklore. Some of the unsubstantiated were that communion wafers bled and that a statue of the Virgin Mary had been miraculously created.[4]

In many cases, the regenerative work simply fell by the wayside. Due to ignorance, superstition, and constricting ecclesiastical protocols, local priests no longer sought the Lord for breakthroughs. Healing became cut off from the everyday life of believers. Christianity's changing paradigms had disastrous ramifications.

Although during this period "prayers for the sick had fallen from regular practice,"[5] it must be reiterated that healing "was practically unbroken for the first thousand years of the church's life."[6] Despite claims to the contrary, physical

---

3. Andrew Daunton-Fear, Healing in the Early Church: The Church's Ministry of Healing and Exorcism from the First to the Fifth Century (Eugene, Oregon: Wipf & Stock, 2009), 157–158.

4. See these claims in Martin Luther, *To the Christian Nobility of the German Nation* (Northport, Alabama: Vision Press, 2017).

5. Wayne Warner, "Faith Healing," Dictionary of Christianity in America (Downers Grove, Illinois: Intervarsity Press, 1990), 424–425.

6. Morton Kelsey, Healing and Christianity in Ancient Thought and Modern Times (New York: Harper and Row, 1973), 6.

deliverance through the auspices of the church "never ceased entirely during the Middle Ages."[7]

In every era, healing is a captivating part of Christian witness. In the face of difficulties and pain, God finds ways to touch the needy. Even in darkness, grace transforms.

---

7. Keith Bailey, Divine Healing: The Children's Bread: God's Provision for Human Health and Healing (Camp Hill, Pennsylvania: Christian Publications, 1977), 211.

Bibliography

For Further Study

Adamnan. *Life of Saint Columba Founder of Hy*, ed. William Reeves. Edinburgh, Scotland: Edmonston and Douglas, 1874. Columba (521–597) was a leader among Irish missionary monks. Exiled from his homeland, he established a monastery at Iona, and from there he spread the gospel to Scotland and Northern England. This work, on his life and miracles, was written in the ninth century.

Aelfric. *Lives of Saints*, 2 volumes, ed. Walter Skeat. London: N. Trübner & Company, 1881. Aelfric (955–1025) was an Anglo-Saxon writer, considered the greatest of his time. His work on the saints was written to provide inspiration and guidance for other monks.

Allen, David. "Signs and Wonders in Bede's History." *Paraclete Journal* 24:4 (Fall 1990): 28–30. Bede's work on the history of the English church was published in the eighth century. This brief essay examines Bede's references to signs, wonders, and healings.

Amundsen, Darrel. *Medicine, Society, and Faith in the Ancient and Medieval Worlds*. Baltimore, Maryland: Johns Hopkins University Press, 2000. In this penetrating work, Amundsen explores the understanding and appropriation of healing in the ancient world.

Ataoguz, Jenny Kirsten. "Visual Preaching in the Early Middle Ages: The Healing Arts at the Carolingian Monastery of

St. John in Müstair, Switzerland," paper presented at the Annual Meeting of the College Art Association, February 2008. In this paper, Ataoguz documents how, around 800 AD, the Church of the Monastery of John the Baptist in Müstair, Switzerland, received an elaborate painting. Meanwhile, a sacramentary and a preaching handbook were composed at the same time. Ataoguz demonstrates how these three items worked together to facilitate ministry. She points out that the strategically-placed cluster of scenes, which depicts Jesus healing, corresponds to healing prayers in the sacramentary, and exhortations in the preaching handbook.

Athanasius. *The Life of Antony and The Letter to Marcellinus*, tr. Robert C. Gregg. Mahwah, New Jersey: Paulist Press, 1979. Athanasius was the celebrated bishop of Alexandria. Around 360, he was asked to write an account of Antony, a mystic, and originator of Christian monasticism. Among other things, Athanasius recounts some healings that took place under Antony's ministry.

Bagnoli, Martina, Holger A. Klein, C. Griffith Mann, and James Robinson, eds. *Treasures of Heaven: Saints, Relics, and Devotion in Medieval Europe*. New Haven: Yale University Press, 2010. This well-researched work explores medieval reliquaries and the individuals that engaged them.

Bartlett, Robert. *Why Can the Dead Do Such Great Things? Saints and Worshippers from the Martyrs to the Reformation.* Princeton, New Jersey: Princeton University Press, 2013. Bartlett, the Bishop Wardlaw Professor of Medieval History at the University of Saint Andrews in Scotland and a fellow of the British Academy, explores the significance of reliquary healing in the medieval church.

Bede. *Ecclesiastical History of the English People*, eds. J.A. Giles and G. Gray. Chicago: Tiger of the Stripe, 2007. The Venerable Bede (AD 672–735) was a historian who documented the expansion of the church in the British Isles. This work that includes several healing accounts, was originally published in 731.

Bonaventure, *The Life of Saint Francis Of Assisi: From* the *"Legenda Santi Francisci of Saint Bonaventure,"* ed. Henry Edward. London: R. Washbourne, 1868. Written shortly after his death, this is the official Franciscan account of Francis Assisi's life and exploits.

Bornstein, Daniel E. "Relics, Ascetics, Living Saints." *A People's History of Christianity: Medieval Christianity*, ed. Daniel E. Bornstein, 75–106. Minneapolis: Fortress Press, 2009. This is a well-researched examination of the meaning of relics in the middle ages.

Brewer, Ebenezer Cobham. *A Dictionary of Miracles, Imitative, Realistic, and Dogmatic.* London: Chatto and Windus, 1901. This book is a compilation of miraculous accounts of early and medieval saints.

Brown, Peter. "Relics and Social Status in the Age of Gregory of Tours." *Society and the Holy in Late Antiquity*, by Peter Brown, 222–250. Berkley, California: University of California Press, 1989. In this academic article, Brown examines healing, relics, and unusual phenomena in the early middle ages.

Brown, Peter. "Society and the Supernatural: A Medieval Change." *Society and the Holy in Late Antiquity.* Berkley, California: University of California Press, 1989. 302–332. In this essay, Brown provides insights into the understanding of the supernatural in the medieval period.

Brown, Peter. *The Cult of the Saints: Its Rise and Function in Latin Christianity.* Chicago: University of Chicago Press, 1981. In this work, Brown explores the role of tombs, shrines, relics, and pilgrimages in the medieval church.

Brown, Peter. "The Rise and Function of the Holy Man in Later Antiquity." *Journal of Roman Studies* 61 (1971): 80–101. This is an article that explores the understanding of the miraculous in the middle ages.

Burgess, Stanley M. *The Holy Spirit: Eastern Christian Traditions.* Peabody, Massachusetts: Hendrickson Publishing, 1989. In this well-researched book, Burgess recounts the understanding and experience of the Holy Spirit in Eastern Church traditions. It includes references to the ministry of healing.

Burgess, Stanley M. *The Holy Spirit: Medieval Roman Catholic and Reformation Traditions.* Peabody, Massachusetts: Hendrickson Publishing, 1997. In this concluding work, Burgess examines medieval and reformed pneumatology. Within these accounts, there are references to healing.

Bulter, Alban. *Butler's Lives of the Saints*, volume 2, eds. Herbert J. Thurston and Donald Attwater. Notre Dame, Indiana: Christian Classics, 1956. Butler (1711-1773), was an English Catholic who, between 1756 and 1759, compiled hundreds of popular accounts of the saints. This work includes several healing accounts.

Bynum, Caroline Walker. *Christian Materiality: An Essay on Religion in Late Medieval Europe.* New York: Zone Books, 2011. This work, from Bynum, clarifies the understanding of healing via relics within the Roman Catholic tradition.

Cardarelli, Sandra and Laura Fenelli. *Saints Miracles and the Image: Healing Saints and Miraculous Images in the Renaissance* (Turnhout, Belgium: Brepols, 2017). This meticulously researched work explores European Roman Catholic healing iconography in the late medieval and early modern period.

Clifton , James James. "Art and Plague at Naples," in *Hope and Healing: Painting in Italy in a Time of Plague*, exh. cat., ed. Gauvin Alexander Bailey and others (Worcester: Clark University, 2005), 97-117. Clifton explores the usage of iconography as source of healing and protection during seasons of plague.

Colgrave, Bertram, ed. and tr. *The Earliest Life of Gregory the Great*. New York: Cambridge University Press, 1968, 1985. Around 700AD, an unknown Anglo-Saxon at Whitby wrote this notable book. It recounts aspects of the life and miracles of Gregory the Great.

Colgrave, Bertram, ed. and tr. *The Life of Bishop Wilfrid by Eddius Stephanus*. New York: Cambridge University Press, 1927, 1985. Stephanus' work, aside from *Bede's Historia Ecclesiastica*, is the only source on Wilfrid. It was written shortly after monk's death in 709. Stephanus recounts a number of Wilfrid's healings and extraordinary events. However, unlike most medieval hagiographies, which consisted of random miracles attributed to saints, this work provides a chronological narrative with specific names and events.

Colgrave, Bertram, ed. and tr. *Two Lives of Saint Cuthbert. New York:* Cambridge University Press, 1940. This is an annotated compilation of two closely associated accounts of Saint Cuthbert of Durham, England (633–687). Both works recount the astounding life and miracles of Cuthbert.

Cornelison, Sally J. and Scott B. Montgomery, eds. *Relics, and Devotional Practice in Medieval and Renaissance Italy* (Tempe, Arizona: Arizona Center for Medieval and Renaissance Studies, 2006). This well researched work explores the meaning and significance of relics in the late medieval and early modern period.

De Voragine, Jacobus. *The Golden Legend: Readings on the Saints*, tr. William Granger Ryan. Princeton, New Jersey: Princeton University Press, 2012. This hagiography was compiled around 1260 by Jacobus de Voragine, a scholarly friar, and archbishop of Genoa. Compiling true and exaggerated accounts of the saints, De Voragine wanted to edify the common people.

Darling, Frank C. *Christian Healing: In The Middle Ages and Beyond*. Boulder, Colorado: Vista Publications, 1990. This historical work briefly explores the history of healing from the middle ages to the present.

Eales, Samuel J. *Saint Bernard, Abbot of Clairvaux, A.D. 1091–1153*. London: Society for Promoting Christian Knowledge, 1890. Bernard (1090–1153) was abbot of the monastery at Clairvaux, and the primary instrument who brought reformation to the Cistercian Order. A number of healings took place through his ministry.

Fenelli, Laura. "Creating a Cult, Faking Relics: The Case of St. Dominic of Soriano," in *Faking, Forging, Counterfeiting: Discredited Practices in the Margins of Mimesis*, ed. Daniel Becker, Annalisa Fiscer, and Yola Schmitz (Bielefeld: Transcript Verlag, 2018), 9-25. This academic paper explores the implications and meaning of a forged relic in the later middle ages.

Finucane, Robert C. "Authorizing the Supernatural: An Examination of English Miracles Around 1318," in *Aspects of Power and Authority in the Middle Ages*, eds. Brenda Bolton and Christine Meek, 289–303. Turnhout: Brepols Publishers, 2007. This is a gripping examination of miracles in late medieval English society.

Finucane, Robert C. "Faith Healing in Medieval England: Miracles at Saints' Shrines," *Psychiatry* 36 (1973): 341–346. This engaging article explores the understanding of reliquary healing in medieval England.

Finucane, Robert C. *Miracles and Pilgrims: Popular Belief in Medieval England.* London: Palgrave Macmillan, 1977. In this work, Ronald C. Finucane analyzes more than 3,000 posthumous accounts of miracles. He pieces together the world of pilgrims, miracles, and faith-healing, demonstrating its hold over the medieval imagination.

Finucane, Robert C. "The Use and Abuse of Medieval Miracles." *History* 60 (1975) 1–10. In this article, Finucane provides some compelling research into the viability of healing during the medieval period.

Floris, Andrew T. "Primacy of the Spiritual." *Paraclete Journal* 6:3 (Summer 1972): 27–32. In this article, Floris deliberates on Symeon, the New Theologian (949–1022), a leader purportedly gifted with great power to operate in healing.

Gardner, Rex. "Miracles of Healing in Anglo-Celtic Northumbria as Recorded by the Venerable Bede and His Contemporaries: A Reappraisal in the Light of Twentieth-Century Experience," *British Medical Journal* 287 (1983): 1927–1933. This is a perceptive article that examines healing accounts in the Venerable Bede's eighth century work.

Goodich, Michael E. *Miracles and Wonders: The Development of the Concept of Miracle, 1150–1350.* Hampshire, United

Kingdom: Ashgate Publishing, 2007. Goodich explores the understanding of miracles in later medieval society.

Greer, Rowan A. *The Fear of Freedom: A Study of Miracles in the Roman Imperial Church.* University Park, Pennsylvania: Penn State University Press, 1989. In this work, Greer explores how miracles shaped catechesis, scriptural exegesis, and piety in the fourth and fifth centuries.

Hildegard of Bingen, *Causae et Curae (Holistic Healing)*, tr. Manfred Pawlik and Patrick Madigan, eds. Mary Palmquist and John Kulas. Collegeville, Minnesota: Liturgical Press, Inc., 1994. Hildegard of Bingen (1098–1179) was a German Benedictine abbess, writer, composer, philosopher, and mystic. *Causae et Curae* is an exploration of the human body, its connections to the natural world, and the causes and cures of various diseases. Hildegard's works are primarily medical, but she often integrates the spiritual. She typically combined physical treatments with holistic methods centered on "spiritual healing."

Hildegard of Bingen. *Physica*, tr. Priscilla Throop. Rochester, Vermont: Healing Arts Press, 1998. *Physica* contains nine books that describe the scientific and medicinal properties of various plants, stones, fish, reptiles, and animals.

Although medical by design, Hildegard refracted these practices through her mysticism.

Heffernan, Thomas J. *Sacred Biography: Saints and Their Biographers in the Middle Ages*. New York: Oxford University Press, 1992. Though medieval collections on the Roman Catholic saints are among the oldest literary texts of Western Christianity, scholars often denigrate them. Heffernan offers a reassessment of the nature and importance of the accounts of the saints, arguing that modern scholarship, bound by its historical-critical methodology, has not understood the underlying principles of these works.

Holmes, Megan. *The Miraculous Image in Renaissance Florence* (New Haven: Yale University Press, 2013). Holmes explores the significance of iconography and relics in the late medieval and early modern period.

Klaniczay, Gábor, "Healing with Certain Conditions: The Pedagogy of Medieval Miracles," Cahiers de recherches médiévales et humanities. *Journal of Medieval and Humanistic Studies* 19 (2010); 235-248. This article explores the understanding of miracles in the later medieval period.

Klaniczay, Gábor, "Using Saints: Intercession, Healing, Sanctity," in *The Oxford Handbook of Medieval*

Christianity, ed. John H. Arnold (Oxford: Oxford University Press, 2014), 217-237. This excellent chapter explores the interrelationship between healing, saints, and relics in medieval Christianity.

Kleinberg, Aviad. *Flesh Made Word: Saints' Stories and The Western Imagination*. Boston: Balknap Press, 2008. Aviad Kleinberg argues that the saints' stories of medieval Europe were more than edifying entertainment: They inspired and created a subversive theology that continues to impact the understanding and practice of Christianity.

Koopmans, Rachel. *Wonderful to Relate: Miracle Stories and Miracle Collecting in High Medieval England*. Philadelphia: University of Pennsylvania Press, 2011. In this work, Rachel Koopmans explores medieval religious culture by examining the miracle stories collected in England from roughly 1080 to 1220.

Kreiser, B. Robert. *Miracles, Convulsions, and Ecclesiastical Politics in Early Eighteenth-Century Paris*. Princeton: Princeton University Press, 1978. Against the backdrop of fierce social and religious conflicts in France, worshipers at the tomb of a Jansenist deacon in Paris' Cemetery of Saint-Médard witnessed a variety of miraculous occurrences.

Kydd, Ronald, A.N. "Jesus, Saints, and Relics: Approaching The Early Church Through Healing." *Journal of Pentecostal Theology* 2 (April 1993): 91–104. This insightful article examines the attitudes and practices of early Christians in matters of healing.

Larchet, Jean-Claude. *Mental Disorders and Spiritual Healing: Teachings from the Early Christian East*, tr. Rama P. Coomaraswamy and G. John Campoux. New York: Sophia Perennis, 1992, 2005. This intriguing volume explores the early Eastern church's understanding of mental illness and demonic affliction. The first chapter, on the Christian valuation of the body, alone is worth the price of the book.

Larchet, Jean-Claude. *The Theology of Illness*. Crestwood: Saint Vladimir's Seminary Press, 2002. This book explores biblical and patristic perspectives on sickness and what some call "redemptive suffering." Larchet, a scholar from the Eastern Orthodox tradition, explores the origin of sin, its impact on physical health, and the healing of human nature by the incarnate Son of God.

Maconachie, C. Leslie. "Anointing and Healing: Truth, Opinion and Misconception: A Study of the Propagation of the Faith in Twelfth Century Britain," Ph.D. diss., Greenwich University, 1990. This work is an exploration

of ritual and healing practices in England during the late
Middle Ages.

Macdougall, Simone. "The Surgeon and the Saints: Henri de
Mondeville on Divine Healing." *Journal of Medieval
History* 26:3 (2000): 253–267. A common theme of
medieval miracle collections was to highlight the
inadequacies of secular medicine while promoting the
divine healing power of the saints. The fourteenth-century
Parisian surgeon Henri de Mondeville provides an
opposing view. Mondeville refutes healing miracles and
the competition that they pose to his profession. He
believes that people should place their confidence in the
operations of the surgeon rather than the intercession of a
saint.

McCready, William D. *Miracles and the Venerable Bede.*
Toronto: Pontifical Institute of Mediaeval Studies, 1994.
This scholarly work carefully examines the healing and
miracle accounts in the *Ecclesiastical History of Bede.*

Moog, Ferdinand Peter, and Axel Karenberg. "St. Francis
came at dawn—the miraculous recovery of a hemiplegic
monk in the Middle Ages." *Journal of Neurological Sciences*
213 (2003): 15–17. The authors of this article present a
case study of a thirteenth-century miracle ascribed to St.
Francis. They draw their report from a detailed summary

of the recovery of a hemiplegic monk whom St. Francis healed through the use of touch.

Nile, Giselle de. *Poetics of Wonder: Testimonies of the New Christian Miracles in the Late Antique Latin World* (Turnhout, Belgium: Brepols, 2012). A resurgence of healings and miracles took in the Latin west, after a centuries-long assumption they had ceased after apostolic times. This work analyzes the reactions to the phenomenon in the extant source material—enthusiasm, puzzlement, deep suspicion, and outright. Nile argues that precept-centered religion gave way to transcendent symbolism.

O'Malley, J. Steven. "Probing the Demise and Recovery of Healing in Christianity." *Pneuma Journal* 5:1 (1983): 46–59. This well-researched article examines the waning of healing after the Nicene Council and attests to its later resurgence.

Patrick. *The Confession of Saint Patrick and Letter to Coroticus*, tr. John Skinner. Colorado Springs, Colorado: Image, 1998. This work is a brief account of St. Patrick's life. It provides a stirring reflection on the miraculous works and healings in Ireland.

Porter, Harry Boone. "The Origins of the Medieval Rite for Anointing the Sick or Dying." *Journal of Theological*

Studies 7:2 (October 1956): 211–225. In this article, Porter explores the history of the last rite as it progressively changes from a sacrament for the sick to a sacrament for the dying.

Renberg, Cil H. *Dreams May Come: Incubation Sanctuaries in the Greco-Roman World* (Leiden and Boston: 2017). Renberg examines the ancient practice of "incubation," the ritual of sleeping at a temple to obtain a prophetic or therapeutic dream. It was originally associated with the Roman healing god Asklepios, but later was utilized in other religious traditions including Christianity.

Scott, Robert A. *Miracle Cures: Saints, Pilgrimage and The Healing Powers of Belief.* Oakland, California: University of California Press, 2010. Using research in biomedical and behavioral science, Scott examines several accounts of miracle cures at medieval, early modern, and contemporary shrines.

Spinks, Jennifer and Dagmar Eichberger, eds. *Religion, Supernatural, and Visual Culture in Early Modern Europe: An album amicorum for Charles Zika* (Leiden and Boston: Brill, 2015). This work explores Roman Catholic materiality and its effect on healing.

Stouck, Mary Ann. "Relics," in *Medieval Saints: Reader*, ed. Mary Ann Stouck, 355–409. Toronto: University of

Toronto Press, 1998. This well-researched entry explores the understanding and scope of relics in the medieval Roman Catholic Church.

Talbot, Charles Hugh, ed. and tr. *The Anglo-Saxon Missionaries in Germany. Being the Lives of SS. Willibrord, Boniface, Sturm, Leoba and Lebuin, Together with the Hodoeporicon of St. Willibald and a Selection from the Correspondence of St. Boniface.* New York: Sheed and Talbot, 1954. This work examines the lives of European missionaries from the early medieval period. It includes a number of healing accounts.

Theodoret of Cyrrhus, *A History of the Monks of Syria*, tr. R.M. Price. Trappist, Kentucky: Cistercian Publications, 1985. This is an important early hagiographic work, documenting Syrian monasticism in the fourth and fifth centuries.

Thunø, Erik, ed. *The Miraculous Image: In the Late Middle Ages and Renaissance* (Rome: L'Erma Di Bretschneider, 2004).This collection of papers sheds light on the visual arts of the Late Middle Ages and the Renaissance,a body of visual material neglected by historians.

Ward, Benedicta. *Miracles and the Medieval Mind: Theory, Record and Event 1000–1215*. Hampshire, England: Wildwood House, 1982, 1987. Ward's study of miracles in the medieval Roman Catholic Church is noteworthy.

Ward, Benedicta. *Signs and Wonders: Saints, Miracles and Prayers from the 4*th *Century to the 14*th. Surrey, England: Ashgate Variorum, 1992. This is, arguably, the seminal work on signs and wonders in the Roman Catholic tradition.

York, William H. *Health and Wellness in Antiquity through the Middle Ages.* Santa Barbara, California: Greenwood, 2012. This academic work explores the diverse health care approaches through different cultures in the ancient world. It also includes reflections on healing practices in the medieval church.

Ziegler, Joseph. "Practitioners and Saints: Medical Men in Canonization Processes in the Thirteenth to Fifteenth Centuries." *Social History of Medicine* 12 (1999): 191–225. In the later middle ages, the church appealed to medical judgment to authenticate miracles. Records of the canonization processes from 1200 – 1500 demonstrate that doctors actively appeared as witnesses in ecclesiastical proceedings.

About J.D. King

J.D. King was a supporting leader in the Smithton Outpouring in the late 1990s. Since then he has also served as an author, pastor, and itinerate speaker.

King spent sixteen years studying the background and theological foundations of healing. The culmination of his research is a three-volume book series called: *Regeneration: The Complete History of Healing in the Christian Church.*

In addition to writing, King guides leaders at the Revival Training Center and serves as a pastor at World Revival Church in Kansas City, Missouri.

To find out more about J.D. and how he could speak to your group, visit him online:

Email: jdking@wrckc.com
Blog: http://authorjdking.com
Bookstore: https://theresurgencestore.com
Twitter: http://twitter.com/jdkinginsights
Facebook: https://www.facebook.com/authorjdking
Newsletter: http://eepurl.com/cVCdQ5

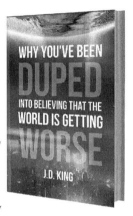

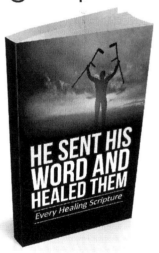

61153907R00090

Made in the USA
Columbia, SC
25 June 2019